Thomas George Bonney

Outline Sketches in the High Alps of Dauphine

Thomas George Bonney

Outline Sketches in the High Alps of Dauphine

ISBN/EAN: 9783743435629

Printed in Europe, USA, Canada, Australia, Japan

Cover: Foto ©ninafisch / pixelio.de

More available books at **www.hansebooks.com**

OUTLINE SKETCHES

IN

THE HIGH ALPS OF DAUPHINÉ.

BY

T. G. BONNEY, M.A. F.G.S.

FELLOW OF S. JOHN'S COLLEGE, CAMBRIDGE;
MEMBER OF THE ALPINE CLUB.

LONDON:
LONGMAN, GREEN, LONGMAN, ROBERTS, & GREEN.
1865.

PREFACE.

I CANNOT let these sketches go forth without a few words of apology for their evident defects. They were drawn simply as records of the scenery and topography of Dauphiné, without any intention of publication; and as I have had neither the time nor the opportunities which are necessary to acquire anything like skill in drawing, I have thought it better not to attempt to make pictures of them, but to leave them nearly in their original condition. Hence some are more elaborate than others, because, when they were made, time or circumstances allowed me to bestow more care upon them; in all, more attention has been given to the outlines of peaks than to the details or arrangement of the foreground. The reason of this is, that my object in making the sketch was to obtain a clear idea of the orography of the country. In the case of some of them another apology may be offered for their faults, namely, that it is not easy to draw when a cold wind is sweeping over the snowfields, when the hand is unsteady after a long climb, or when considerable attention has to be given to the maintenance of equilibrium. I trust, however, that they may serve to draw the attention of tourists to scenes, the beauty of which is rarely equalled and, perhaps, never surpassed by any other part of the Alps.

Much of the text has already been published in one form or another. I have therefore, at the risk of dulness, for the most part, excluded incidents of travel, and confined myself to a simple description of the topography and scenery of the country, and to giving such information as a traveller would need. Hence the book will chiefly be useful to those who, like myself, are never quite contented with an Alpine view, however beautiful, until they are able to identify every summit in it.

I cannot conclude without expressing my thanks to Mr. Adlard for the pains which he has taken in making fac-similes of my sketches; to my friends, Messrs. W. Mathews, Tuckett, and E. Walton, for advice and assistance in the work; and to my travelling companions for many pleasant days of social intercourse among the scenes herein described, the memory of which will not easily be effaced.

T. G. BONNEY.

S. JOHN'S COLLEGE, CAMBRIDGE:
    December 15, 1864.

CONTENTS.

DESCRIPTION OF THE PLATES.

INTRODUCTION.

THE GROUP OF MOUNTAINS which this little volume is designed to illustrate lies in the irregular triangle formed by the valleys of the Romanche on the north, the Durance on the east, and the Drac on the south-west. The glacier-bearing peaks do not, however, occupy the whole of this area, but are crowded together in the north-eastern angle, where the narrow ridge of the Combaynou, rising between the Col du Lautaret and Col des Arsines, like a bridge connects this huge outpost with the main chain of the Alps. Though the summits of Dauphiné are lower than those of the Pennine range, and its glaciers less extensive than the icefields of the Oberland, it surpasses every other district in the Western and Central Alps in the savage grandeur of its precipices and the almost fantastic outlines of its peaks. There are four mountains between 14,000 ft. and 13,000 ft. and seventeen between 13,000 ft. and 12,000 ft.; fourteen passes exceeding 10,000 ft. have already been discovered, and its glaciers, including those of the second order, are more than one hundred. East of this group, on the opposite side of the Durance, rises the main chain of the Cottian Alps, and north of it runs a large spur, which, starting from Mount Tabor, divides the valley of the Romanche from that of the Arc, and widens out into the mountain mass forming for some distance the eastern boundary of the Isère. In the former of these two ranges there is no peak [1] which can at all vie with

[1] The pyramidal summit of the Roche-brune, or Bouchier, 10,906 ft. (Joanne, ii. 235), is the highest point in this part of the Cottian chain. It is visible from the east side of the Lautaret road, and from Monétier over the forts of Briançon.

those of the outlying group; and in the latter only the craggy heads of
the Aiguilles d'Arve, and the two highest teeth of the Grandes Rousses
exceed 11,000 ft.   The ground-plan of the central district is that of a
loop, enclosing the Vénéon and defined by the valleys of the Romanche,
Guisanne, Vallouise with its tributaries, Godemar and Jouffrey.   It
consists of a mass of metamorphic rock, in which protogine gneiss is an
important constituent, that has been thrust up through the overlying
liassic strata, which, contorted and crumpled by the pressure of the
extruded area, now rest in a highly-inclined position on its flanks.
Beside this crystalline nucleus, two long spurs, starting from near its
western extremity, break through the sedimentary rocks, the smaller
forming the serrate ridge of the Grandes Rousses, the latter running in
a north-east direction from the mouth of the Val Jouffrey almost up to
Mont Blanc.   The valley of the Romanche gives an excellent transverse
section of the northern part of the district.   The traveller, on emerging
from among the crystalline cliffs of the Combe de Gavet, sees before him
on the left bank of the Olle the shales and limestone bands of the sedimentary deposits which occupy the trough between the two above-named
ridges.   As he approaches Bourg he will perceive (on the right bank of the
Romanche) the crystalline rocks gradually rising again from below and
bearing up with them the sedimentary deposits, which rest on them
unconformably.   After quitting the cirque of Bourg the road follows a
narrow rift in the crystalline rock, until on nearing Freney the trough of
sedimentary strata, which runs right across the country by the Col de
Venos to the Col de la Muzelle, is again intersected.[1]   The crystalline
rock, however, soon rises again, and no more is seen of the slates until,
after the Combe de Malaval is quitted, they again cross the river near La
Grave, at which place the road runs for some distance over them.   After
following the Romanche still further towards its source, the crystalline
rock reappears in the bed of the river, on the way to the Col des Arsines.

[1] My impression is that the bed of the Romanche is almost continuously of the
crystalline rock even here.

A few words may now be said on the general orography of the central mass, which, as I have said, forms a kind of loop or horse-shoe around the Venéon.[1] The western end of the northern arm of this rises boldly above the junction of the Romanche and Venéon in a fine craggy peak, probably not much less than 9,000 ft. high. Next to this is a depression, called the Col de Venos, from which the range rises till it forms a vast plateau, sloping to the north-west, covered by the Glacier du Mont de Lans. Beyond this is the ridge of the Râteau, 12,369 ft.; then the jagged crête of the Meije or Aiguille du Midi de la Grave, terminating in a huge glacier-covered buttress on the north-east. The line of the water-shed now turns southward, and, after dropping down to the Col de la Cavale, rises in the Grande Ruine to a height of 12,316 ft. From this a short spur runs eastward. A high ridge joins the Grande Ruine to the Sommet de Roche-Faurio, from which another long spur, called the Crête du Glacier Blanc, runs eastward, rising near its extremity to a height of 12,008 ft. After the Roche-Faurio, the main chain sinks down to a height of about 11,000 ft. at the Col des Ecrins, and then rises rapidly to the Pointe des Ecrins, the monarch of the group. This may be described as a triangular pyramid, two sides being nearly vertical rock and the third a steep slope of snow. It has two distinct summits, the lower a dome of snow 13,058 ft., the other a sharp rocky triangle, the apex of which is 13,462 ft. above the sea, with a knob on the northern arête, considered as a separate peak, whose height is 13,396 ft. To the south of Les Ecrins is the Crête de la Bérarde, 12,323 ft., then the huge wedge of the Ailefroide, 12,878 ft., lying nearly east and west, from which runs a spur terminating in the truncated cone of the Pelvoux, 12,973 ft., with two intermediate peaks, respectively 11,772 ft. (?) and 12,845 ft. Beyond the Ailefroide the line of the watershed runs southward for a short distance, dividing the Glacier de la Pilatte from the Glacier du Sélé, and then sweeps round so as completely to enclose the former. The rugged mass

[1] See Map, and Plates II. III. VIII. IX.

between the Vallons de la Pilatte and de la Muande has several peaks between 11,000 ft. and 12,000 ft., the highest of which is the Sommet des Rouies, 11,923 ft., overhanging the Col de la Muande. From this pass the ridge runs in a north-west direction, having several mountains rather lower than those just named, the highest being the Pic d'Olan, 11,739 ft.; and the line of glacier-bearing peaks may be considered as terminating at the Rocher de Rochail, 10,070 ft., above the little glacier of Villard Eymond. Inside the loop the Râteau throws off a craggy spur, dividing the Vallon de la Selle from the Vallon des Etançons, one point of which, the Aiguille du Plat, reaches a height of 11,818 ft.[1] In the northern half of the loop the mountains are generally more precipitous on their inner side, while the contrary is the case in the southern. Hence in either case the glaciers on the northern slope generally extend to the top of a pass, while on the southern they are separated from it by a wall of snow or rock. The precipitous character of the mountains renders climbing among them for the most part laborious and difficult, and from the same reasons the glaciers are often very much broken; hence they are sometimes only practicable in the early part of the summer, while their crevasses are still bridged by the unmelted winter snow. The traveller often longs in vain for the pleasant alps and pinewood paths that generally await him in other places when he has descended to a height of from 7,000 to 8,000 feet. Here precipices or steep slopes of broken rock, lying in every position of unstable equilibrium, continue to the very last; and in making a new pass the difficulties cannot be considered as over till the stream in the valley is reached.

Another great drawback on travelling in Dauphiné is the bad accommodation to be met with in the inns. A good digestion and an insect-proof skin are indispensable requisites to any one wishing to explore comfortably the less frequented districts. As unfortunately I possess

---

[1] I do not think that there is any communication between the Glaciers de la Selle and des Etançons, as would appear from the French map; at any rate, I have been unable to get a sight of the snowfield.

neither the one nor the other, I have never been able to make a long stay in the country, and have always suffered more or less for my visit. On the great high road from Grenoble to Briançon there is fair accommodation at one or two places. Off this everything is of the poorest kind; fresh meat can only be obtained at rare intervals, the bread and wine are equally sour, the auberges filthy, and the beds entomological vivaria. It is hardly possible to conceive the squalid misery in which the people live; their dark dismal huts swarming with flies, fleas, and other vermin; the broom, the mop, and the scrubbing-brush are unknown luxuries; the bones and refuse of a meal are flung upon the floor to be gnawed by the dogs, and are left there to form an osseous breccia. The people in many parts are stunted, cowardly, and feeble, and appear to be stupid and almost *crétins*. Too often there, as in other parts of the Alps, 'every prospect pleases, and only man is vile.'

Despite, however, of all this, I do not hesitate to call Dauphiné the most interesting district in the Alps, and as a whole superior in both the beauty and the grandeur of its scenery to any other mountain group with which I am acquainted. Its position, so far to the south of the other glacier-bearing areas of the Alps, renders the temperature of its valleys much higher than that which prevails in similar positions farther north, and consequently gives a greater variety to its flora. The botanist and entomologist will reap a rich harvest; and even those who, like myself, are ignorant of the former science, will be delighted by the beauty and profusion of its wild flowers. But on these points it is not my purpose to enlarge; I must refer my reader to the treatises published by various scientific Frenchmen, many of which are enumerated in the 'Alpine Guide' (Western Alps).

THE HIGH ALPS

OF

DAUPHINÉ.

———◦⊙◦———

CHAPTER I.

JOURNEY OF 1860.

GRENOBLE—COMBE DE GAVET—BOURG D'OISANS—VENOS—ST. CHRISTOPHE—LA BÉRARDE,
L'AILEFROIDE AND THE COL DE SAIS—RETURN TO BOURG—BRIANÇON—THE VALLOUISE—
UNSUCCESSFUL ATTEMPT ON THE PELVOUX—GUILESTRE.

MOST TRAVELLERS will, I think, admit that there is a charm in novelty,
and that a certain zest is given to the pleasure derived from the beauties
of nature by the knowledge that they have been seldom or never seen
by others. It was this pardonably selfish feeling which induced Mr. J. C.
Hawkshaw and myself to include a visit to the Alps of Dauphiné in our
programme for a holiday ramble in the summer of 1860. The same
spirit had infected our friend Mr. W. Mathews jun., who, on learning
our intentions, kindly agreed to defer his tour until we could join
him. La Bérarde was to be our rendezvous (on the 12th of August),
whither he was to go *vid* the Tarentaise and Maurienne, we direct
from England. Before starting, we of course endeavoured to get all
the information possible concerning the district. The ordinary guide-
books and maps were useless; the fascinating article affixed to ' Norway

B

and its Glaciers,' and a few notes from one or two friends who had just
dipped into the country, were all that we could meet with in the way of
instructions; while maps were a still greater difficulty. The common
atlases did not recognise the existence of mountains in that part of
France. A few, better instructed, put some feeble suggestive scratches
between the Romanche and Durance, attaching thereto the name 'Mont
Pelvoux.' Bourcet's large 'Carte Géometrique du Haut Dauphiné' was
the only one with any pretence to accuracy, and this was obviously vague
above the snow-line. Our ideas, therefore, of the country were neces-
sarily hazy; so we went to La Bérarde in the hope of enlightening
them, and of examining the Pelvoux, which we believed (erroneously)
to overhang the valley a short distance above that hamlet.

Leaving Lyons early on the morning of August 10th, Hawkshaw
and I quitted the main line at St. Rambert, and took the branch
railway for Grenoble. The portals of the Alps are generally striking, and
this approach to Dauphiné is no exception to the rule. After passing
Voreppe, towering hills with limestone precipices, rendered vaster by
wreaths of mist clinging to their crags, seemed to close in upon the
railway, till on sweeping round a curve we caught sight of the town,
built on a little plain by the Isère. Up the hill on the left crept serpent-
like a covered way of stone, connecting two grey massive forts which
defend this entrance into France. Above, their flanks veiled in clouds
and their crests streaked with snow, rose a billowy chain of peaks,
a fine background to the picture. We had no time to lose, so after
getting some lunch at the Hôtel des Trois Dauphins (a dingy place
where Napoleon lodged on his return from Elba), we engaged a carriage
and started for Bourg d'Oisans. For some miles the bed of the valley
is a dead flat, and this, with the pouring rain, made the first part of
our journey sufficiently monotonous. Presently the junction of the Drac
and the Romanche is reached, and the road then keeps near the latter
river, which testifies by its wide débris-strewn bed what its violence
is in time of flood. Passing through Vizille, with its grim château,

once the home of Lesdiguières, now a factory, we reached Séchilienne, near the entrance of the Combe de Gavet. Fortunately, the rain had ceased for a time, so that we had a good view of the noted valley. At first the hills on the left, though bleak and steep, are not very precipitous; those on the right, though more craggy, are masked by a luxuriant growth of brushwood which starts from every cranny. Further on the scene becomes wilder, the mountains higher and bolder, pines begin to appear, and huge blocks fallen from above almost overhang the road. The grandeur of the view was heightened by the cloud wreaths that crept along the mountain sides or clung around their summits. At a place near the junction of two ravines, one of which descends from the Pointe de l'Infernet on the right, and the other from the Voudène on the left, a vast mass of débris, chiefly brought down by an *éboulement* from the latter mountain, formerly obstructed the course of the Romanche, and converted the plain of Oisans into a lake. This was in the twelfth century, and so it remained until the night of September 14, 1219, when the barrier burst, and the waters rushed down to Grenoble, sweeping away everything before them. The year before we passed, the road had been destroyed, and the Romanche stopped for half an hour by a similar, though happily a smaller, landslip. The crags of the Voudène, with a waterfall looking through the mist like a spectral giant horsetail, were magnificent. After quitting the Combe, we came out upon the fertile plain at the junction of the Olle and Romanche, above which huge precipices of banded limestone and shale were dimly looming through the evening mists. It was quite dark and the rain was falling fast when we drove up to the doors of the Hôtel de Milan at Bourg d'Oisans, where we found very fair accommodation.

It was no small relief, when we woke the next morning, to see the sun shining brightly and the mist rolling up the mountains with every promise of a brilliant day. Breakfast, rendered luxurious by some splendid trout from the Lac de Lauvitel, being despatched, we extricated ourselves from the town and got on to the road leading to Venos. Bourg

stands on the level plain at the confluence of the Romanche and the
Venéon. Looking back, the craggy summits of the Belledonne appear
frowning over the Combe de Gavet and the valley of the Olle. To this
succeeds a mass of grey and purple banded rock, from below which rises
the crystalline ridge that culminates in the Grandes Rousses, one of whose
snowy peaks may be seen in the distance. A stream from its glaciers
has swept away the sedimentary slates from one side of the glen down
which it rushes, and sawn a deep gorge in the metamorphic rock below,
whence it rushes in a cascade. The boundary of the denuded area can
be traced far up the glen, by the sudden change from bare stony alps to
cornfields and rich pastures.

The Romanche enters the cirque of Bourg by a ravine so narrow as to
be hardly discerned, while the valley of the Venéon is comparatively
wide and open. The hills on each side of it are bold and rocky, but only
the outposts of their snows, the little glaciers of Lauvitel and Villard, are
visible. A dreary tract of sand and pebbles has to be crossed before the
Combe de Venos is entered, but when once the right bank of that valley
is reached the walk is very pleasant. The slopes of broken rock below
the cliffs are almost masked by lavender plants, which scent the air and
afford a paradise to innumerable butterflies. Presently appear the
snows of the Roche de la Muzelle, and of the Tête de l'Être; then a
steep ascent leads up to the village of Venos, embosomed in walnut-trees,
an oasis of slate in a desert of crystalline rock. We turned into the
village inn, chez Paquet, for lunch. Oleanders flourished in the balcony,
and some quaint antique furniture adorned the rooms. Madame Paquet, a
comfortable looking old dame, did her best for us, and we went on our
way well pleased with our entertainment. Beyond Venos is the Clapier
de St. Christophe, a desolate scene of ruin caused by the fall of a mountain
peak into the narrow gorge. The road winds amidst huge blocks piled
pell-mell one on another, the torrent frets and roars among them far
below, while the unstained splinters and the fresh seams on the scarred
and barren mountain sides shew that a like accident may occur again.

At the wildest spot the road crosses the stream by a natural bridge formed of huge slabs. The path then, after traversing a gravelly flat, mounts a hill to avoid a deep gorge. St. Christophe is now seen, but a descent to the level of the Torrent du Diable, and another ascent, must be made before the village is reached. The inn was poor and dirty, but a small upper chamber, approached by a flight of steps on the other side of the road, was allotted to us, so after a little arrangement we did pretty well. Meat was not to be got, but eggs, honey, &c. were plentiful. Not wishing to tire ourselves, we halted here, and spent the rest of the day in strolling about. A fine series of cascades, formed by the above-named torrent, will well repay a visit. The best point of view is but a short distance above the road. Our room commanded a beautiful prospect of the Tête de l'Être, and the other mountains east of the Combe de la Muande,[1] so we found ample employment for our pencils.

Next morning it rained so hard that our sole amusement was watching a wedding procession walk to church under huge red umbrellas. Much powder was burnt, and a sheep was killed in honour of the happy couple; so we got a leg of mutton for dinner. In the afternoon we started for La Bérarde, and, though the rain did not cease for some time, we got some views of the magnificent cliffs forming the north-east boundary of the Vallon de Venéon. The precipices of Les Ecrins, as seen from the little village of Les Etages are magnificent.[2]

La Bérarde is a miserable hamlet, built at the junction of the Vallon des Etançons with the main valley. Fowls and goats, pigs and people, occupy harmoniously the squalid huts, and the cows are as well lodged as their masters. We had been directed to the best house, that belonging to Rodier, formerly guide to Principal Forbes. The family consisted of this worthy, clad in a mangy sheepskin suit, his wife, their son and his wife, a naked baby safely strapped down in a cradle, and two or three older brats, all uniformly dirty. The cottage had but one room, and

---

[1] Engraved in 'Peaks, Passes, and Glaciers,' second series, vol. ii. p. 203.
[2] See plate in 'Norway and its Glaciers,' p. 270; also 'Alpine Guide,' vol. i. p. 75.

the sleeping accommodation consisted of two beds in the wall, like cup-
boards without doors, with drawers below in which, as I ascertained in
1863, the children reposed. Mathews did not appear; so we determined
to wait a day, and spend it in reconnoitring the neighbourhood. We
accordingly took counsel with Rodier junior, and were not a little sur-
prised at the value that he set upon his services. Under fifteen francs a
day he would not stir; for crossing a glacier pass he demanded forty-five
francs; and half the sum for going to a col and returning. Of course we
remonstrated, but in vain; so after a long wrangle we engaged him to
go with us on the morrow to the Col de Sais,[1] choosing this because we
thought it ought to command a good view of the Pelvoux.

We slept, or rather lay still to be devoured, in a separate room called
the grange, among straw, tools, shelves of black bread, and other 'notions.'
The morning, though cloudy, was cold; at 6.20 we started and walked
rapidly up the valley to the foot of the Glacier de la Pilatte. As we
saw little of the scenery on this occasion, I shall leave the description of
this part of the excursion for another time, and merely state that we
soon ascertained from Rodier that the magnificent craggy peak which
we had come out to examine was not the Pelvoux, but quite a different
mountain, bearing the name of L'Ailefroide. The glacier is formed by
the union of two ice-streams, one draining a large amphitheatre under
the crags of the Ailefroide and the Crête des Bœufs Rouges, the other
descending from the (eastern) Col de Sais; these are divided by a buttress
of rock which is crowned by a snowy peak. Getting on the ice without
difficulty, we bore to the right, crossing many old snow-beds, the remains
of avalanches, until we came near the foot of the ice-fall of the second
glacier. We then took to the rocks on its left bank; these, being rather
steep and abounding in loose stones, masked with fresh snow, required
some care; nevertheless we worked steadily on until we found ourselves
above the worst part of the fall and nearly on a level with the upper
basin of the glacier. It was, however, still intersected with some ugly-

[1] Two passes bear this name; the eastern, here described, and the western, at the
head of the Glacier du Chardon.

looking crevasses, partially concealed by snow. Here Rodier informed us that owing to these we could go no further. We confessed ourselves unable to see the force of his argument and suggested the use of the rope, which we had ordered him to bring. He then produced, to our disgust, a common mule rope about twelve feet long. This was by no means satisfactory, but as we had no intention of returning we set to work to find our way through the crevasses, and before long spied the track of a chamois, threading the maze. Following this, carefully sounding as we went, we cleared the chasms and then addressed ourselves to the snow slopes beyond. Here again Rodier stopped, saying that he was tired, so we administered brandy and sent him to the rear; after which we divided the rest of the work between ourselves, and reached the col at eleven.

The view thence is very fine; in front, the eye, after glancing over a short slope of snow, rests upon the pines and pastures, many thousand feet below, at the head of the Val Godemar, on the other side of which rises a fine mass of dark crags and couloirs of snow. Beyond this are seen several ranges of hills stretching away into the distance, streaked here and there with snow, but without any prominent peak. Behind, across the narrow rift of the Vallon de Clotchâtel, towers the Ailefroide, rising in a series of almost vertical precipices, and culminating in·one flame-like point nearly seven thousand feet above the bed of the valley. On its left are the Crête de la Bérarde and the Ecrins; but the latter, though really the highest summit of the group, is quite dwarfed by distance. It was too cold to linger, so after a hasty sketch[1] we hurried down the snow slopes, retraced our steps cautiously among the crevasses, and after descending the rocks arrived in good time at La Bérarde. Here we had the pleasure of finding Mathews, who had been delayed by the bad weather, and had walked up from Venos that morning, having crossed the Col de Venos in the rain the day before. He was accompanied by his guide Michel A. Croz, who was then on his travels for the first time.

[1] Engraved in 'Peaks, Passes, and Glaciers,' second series, vol. ii. p. 209.

After reporting the results of our exploration, we arranged to cross to the Valloise by the Col de la Tempe on the morrow, after only partially defeating an ingenious attempt at imposition on the part of the Rodiers, *père et fils*. For variety, we tried the hayloft as a sleeping chamber. It would have been less interesting to an entomologist than our previous quarters, but was more agreeable to wearied travellers.

Next morning we woke up to a dismal consciousness of rain and mist. The col was hopeless. Another day at La Bérarde, and that a wet one, was too dismal a prospect to be endured; so we shouldered our knapsacks and marched doggedly and disgustedly to Bourg d'Oisans, where we arrived in due course, somewhat tired and ravenously hungry, as we had not halted to rest or eat on the way.

The next day we drove by La Grave over the Lautaret to Briançon. As the clouds hung low on the mountains, and as I have since passed over nearly the whole of the road under more favourable circumstances, I shall not describe it at present. Briançon is a picturesquely situated town, well worth a visit. Bartlett[1] and Brockedon[2] have employed their pencils upon its beauties, so I forbear to enlarge upon them. We found the town itself rather close and noisy, and the Hôtel de la Paix neither clean nor comfortable.

Next morning we drove before breakfast to La Bessée, a stage of about two hours. It is opposite to the entrance of the Vallouise, and commands a fine view of the Pelvoux and some of the other summits in the vicinity. Let me, however, advise the reader not to depend upon the auberge for a meal; our hopes were cruelly blighted. Our intentions with regard to the Pelvoux had become known, and before leaving we were visited by M. Jean Reynaud, *agent-voyer* of the district, who requested us to allow him to join our party. We accordingly started together for Ville de Vallouise, where we hoped to find some one acquainted with the mountain. Unfortunately the clouds had by this time fallen upon

[1] 'The Waldenses.'   [2] 'Passes of the Alps,' vol. i.

the summits, so that we were unable to make any sketches, or reconnoitre
in any way. At Ville we learnt that we should find a guide at Claux,
the next village, and should have to pass the night at the 'Cabane des
Bergers de Provence.' Supposing that this was a châlet, we left our
knapsacks at the auberge and walked on, followed by a porter carrying
as good a stock of provisions as we could get. At Claux we fell in with
the guide, Joseph Semiond by name, who professed that he knew the
mountain well, and consented to go with us if we would let him bring
his brother. Increased in number to eight, we followed the rough path to
the châlets of Ailefroide, which stand on a little open plain at the junction
of the valleys Sapenière and St. Pierre, at the very foot of the Pelvoux.
Here we dismissed our porter, and halted to refresh on black bread and
milk. The former of these two native products is baked once or twice a
year in round flat cakes; consequently it is as hard as a board. Soaked
in milk it is not bad, but when eaten alone it resembles a mouthful of
mahogany sawdust more than anything else that I know.

On quitting the châlet, we followed the Val Sapenière for a short
distance, and then turned up towards a steep gorge on the right. A
scramble over broken rocks led us to the foot of the cliffs, up which we
climbed by a narrow goat track, that was at best a poor apology for a
path, until after about an hour and a half we came out upon some turf
slopes, sprinkled over with fragments of rock, to one of which the
guide pointed, saying 'Voilà la cabane.' Alas for the visions of fresh
hay and hospitable bergers! It was but a huge block that had fallen
from the cliffs above, and formed a sort of kennel, which had been
improved by a wall of 'dry masonry' in the regular style of Celtic
hill forts. For hay there was a mixture of damp clay and stones, for
bergers a dead sheep in a lively condition. This soon went over the
cliffs for the ravens, and while our guides were cleansing out the place
we had leisure to look around us. It was a strange wild scene.
Overhead hung the crags of the Pelvoux splintered into flame-like points;
from their feet sloped down vast banks of fallen blocks, overgrown with

serpent-like branches of old junipers, and broken here and there by
slopes of turf. A few feet in front of our cave steep precipices overhanging the fatal Balme[1] led down to the valley below, across which
rose another mass of rocks and pine-covered slopes, surmounted by a
ridge of cliffs somewhat overtopping us; while a fine pyramidal peak, from
which a large glacier (Sélé) descended, closed the head of the valley.[2]

The increasing cold soon drove us within the cave, and the night was
passed in trying to solve the following problem: ' Given some clay for a
mattress, a stone for a pillow, and juniper smoke for an atmosphere, how
to sleep?' Morning did but reveal mist and rain, and the Pelvoux was
obviously impossible. However, we had come too far to be easily beaten
off, so we determined to stay where we were. Accordingly we sent our
guides down to Ville for some more provisions, and spent the day in
endeavouring, like Mark Tapley, to be jolly under difficulties. I must
confess that we were not very successful, though we escaped the lowest
depth of quarrelling for employment. The rain abated sufficiently
towards evening to allow us to take a short stroll and gather some wood
for the night. Among other defects in our mansion was a perviousness
to water, due to certain cracks in the roof. Hence the floor had become
too wet for us to lie on, so we half sat, half reclined on stones all night,
with our legs in a tangled heap near the fire. The effect of all this was,
that when I woke up it was some time before I discovered which were
really my own limbs.

The weather, hateful word, was rather more promising next morning,
so about four we started. At first we kept nearly on the same level,
advancing towards the Glacier du Sélé, until we reached a wide open
gorge communicating with the valley below. Then we turned upwards,
and soon exchanged the turf for a steep slope of fallen rocks that separated
us from the cliffs. On reaching these our work began. There was

[1] A cavern in which a number of Vaudois
are said to have been suffocated by fires
lighted outside, A.D. 1488.

[2] Plate I. No. IV. It is the extremity of
a spur of the Ailefroide. The Col du Sélé
lies just behind it.

much fresh snow and ice on the ledges, so that care was required. We
climbed steadily up steep crags, varied now and then by a hard couloir
of snow. It was rather monotonous work, the only distraction being
an occasional glance at the wide expanse of serrate peaks to the south-
east, from among which the great pyramid of the Viso rose like an island
mountain out of a stormy sea.

The clouds, however, began to gather and blot out the prospect, and
the local guides to murmur ominously. When we halted for breakfast
the second man declared himself exhausted and unable to proceed
further; so we dismissed him. The other soon began to talk about
stopping, and at last, on arriving at the side of a small glacier, he refused
to proceed further, talking vaguely of all imaginable dangers. Blandish-
ments and abuse were tried equally in vain; even money seemed to
have lost its charms; he would lead us no longer. The mist, though
insufficient to justify his turning back, was too thick to make it possible
for us, without the least topographical knowledge, to continue our
expedition; so with heavy hearts we descended, vituperating the
unfortunate natives, and revenging ourselves upon them by racing down
the aforesaid gorge to the bottom of the valley. The character of the
descent, over a genuine Dauphiné *clapier*, made it an admirable substitute
for Mr. Weller sen.'s celebrated receipt for shaking the nonsense out of
lazy shepherds.

After lunch and a siesta by the stream, we walked down the valley to
Ailefroide, and thence to Ville de Vallouise. Here we parted from
M. Reynaud, with regret at losing so pleasant and genial a companion,
and withal so good a walker. Then we descended as fast as possible to
La Bessée, where we hired a carriage and drove in the dusk to Guilestre.
Here, at the Hôtel des Alpes, we were in comparative luxury, and if my
reader wants to get a thorough appreciation of the comfort of a bed, I
can confidently prescribe for him two nights out on the rocks, and a long
walk by day.

Next morning we left in a carriage for Abriès. On our way through the town we looked into the church, which is well worth a visit. There is a fine porch of three arches, supported on slender columns of mottled red marble (obtained in the vicinity), which rest on the backs of animals. It resembles those common in the north of Italy. From the road, a little above the town, we got a view of the Pelvoux, and of some parts of the neighbouring mountains ; but there were so many clouds about that we were not able to learn much. For the scenery of the Combe de Queyras and the neighbourhood of the Viso I must refer my reader to the works which have already been published on this district ; for ourselves, suffice it to say that, after two or three days more of bad weather, we escaped over the Col de Seylières (9,247 ft.) to Turin.

CHAPTER II.

COL DE MAURIN—COL DE CHISTILLAN—GUILESTRE—VALLOUISE—NIGHT BY THE
GLACIER BLANC—ATTEMPT ON LES ECRINS—COL DU GLACIER BLANC.

In 1861 I was prevented from visiting Dauphiné, but interest had been
excited in the district, and Messrs. Whymper and Macdonald, favoured
by fine weather, after one failure due to the local guide, followed
their own course and climbed the Pelvoux. In the spring of 1862
appeared the second series of ' Peaks, Passes, and Glaciers,' into which all
the information was incorporated that could be gathered together about
Dauphiné. Owing to the badness of the maps, the unpropitious weather
from which most of the explorers had suffered, and an unfortunate mistake
made by Mr. Whymper in identifying the mountains near the Pelvoux,
the result of our labours was still vague and unsatisfactory. Accordingly
Mr. Tuckett determined to visit the group, and as he fortunately succeeded in obtaining a copy of the unpublished MS. map, prepared by the
officers of the État-Major Français, and was favoured with tolerable
weather, he was able to make several snow excursions of the highest
interest and to clear up much of the geography of the district. On his
return to England he wrote to Mathews, announcing his most important
discovery, that the Pointe des Arsines or Ecrins, the highest summit of
Dauphiné, was not, as had hitherto been supposed, a part of the Pelvoux,
but a mountain at the head of the Glacier Blanc, identical with the
Montagne d'Oursine of the neighbourhood of La Bérarde. At the same
time he sent one of his admirable outline sketches with the probable route

to the summit indicated, and full instructions about the best mode of making the attack.

Accordingly, Mathews and I, accompanied by our guides, Jean Baptiste and Michel Croz, determined to return home from our tour in the Tarentaise and Gruians *viâ* Turin; and, after being again driven from the Viso by bad weather, we crossed into France by the Col de Maurin, at the head of the valley of the Ubaye, and then, after descending a short distance, bore away to the right and reached the summit of the Col de Cristillan. Hence we had a noble panorama of the Pelvoux range; and as I was then unaware how thoroughly Mr. Tuckett had explored the group, I determined to seize every opportunity of sketching it. This I have always found the best way of learning mountain geography: it matters little how rude the drawings are, provided the main features are given with tolerable correctness. Plates II. and III. represent the view as seen from the Col. The mountain (1) on the extreme left in Plate II. is Mont Bans, the highest point in the Crête des Bœufs Rouges; it is seen from near La Bérarde.[1] The glaciers to the right lie on the north side of the Vallon des Bancs; below (2) is the Col du Sélé from La Bérarde to Ailefroide by the glaciers of La Pilatte and Sélé; (3) is the Ailefroide, its glaciers streaming down towards the Val de Sapenière to join that last mentioned; (4) is a point in the ridge joining the Ailefroide to the Pelvoux; (5) is a summit which deserves a better name than the vague term Crête du Pelvoux. Then comes the Pelvoux, shewing the little glacier of Clôt de l'Homme, by the side of which we were obliged to stop. In Plate III. (1) is the highest summit of the Pelvoux; (2) is the Pic de la Pyramide, on which the French engineers spent several days when engaged on the survey; (3) is the summit of Les Écrins, with the Crête de l'Encula on the right overhanging the Glacier Noir. Round the Crête sweeps the Glacier Blanc. (4) marks pretty nearly the position of the Col du Glacier Blanc, from Ailefroide to La Grave, discovered by Mr. Tuckett. (5) is

---

[1] 'Peaks, Passes, and Glaciers,' second series, vol. ii. p. 189.

the Meije, or Aiguille du Midi de la Grave, seen over the Crête du Glacier Blanc, the highest points of which, sometimes called the Mountains of Monêtier (6), are seen to the right. Further to the right lay a bank of clouds, over which the double-headed Aiguilles d'Arve towered grimly, and in the distance rose the Grandes Rousses, some of the summits of the Tarentaise, and Mont Blanc.

A steep slope of loose stones leads from the col to the pastures at the head of the valley, the upper part of which is barren and uninteresting, but the road is good and descends at an easy gradient. After about two hours' walking we entered a small but pretty combe, the portal to better scenery. From Ceillac, a fair-sized village about a mile farther on, is a fine view of a snow mountain (Pointe des Orches?) at the head of another arm of the valley. The scenery for the rest of the walk, until the main road in the valley of the Guil is reached, resembles that of the Combe de Queyras, but is not on quite so grand a scale. The entrance to the valley of Ceillac from that of the Guil is so narrow, and on a so much higher level, that the passing traveller would not suppose it to be more than a mere glen.

We now rapidly descended the excellent carriage road to Guilestre and soon were delighted to see the magnificent forms of the Pelvoux group rising again before us; no longer, as on a former occasion, half veiled in clouds. Knowing how transitory such good fortune is, I seated myself by the roadside at the first convenient spot and made a careful outline,[1] while my companions walked on to secure beds at the hotel.

From the immediate neighbourhood of Guilestre the same view may be seen, together with part of the Crête de l'Encula and a considerable portion of the Crête du Glacier Blanc. Plate V. No. III. is an outline of this addition to the view. The Col du Glacier Blanc may be readily recognised by a round patch of rock protruding from a smooth glacier. After dinner we took a carriage and drove by Mont Dauphin, perched

[1] Plate IV

above picturesque crags and pillars of conglomerate rock, to La Bessée; and thence, after spending a pleasant hour with M. Reynaud, to Ville de Vallouise. Just before reaching that village there is a fine view of the crags and glaciers of the Vallon des Bancs, which leads to the Col du Célar. The *salle* of Giraud's little inn was occupied by peasants keeping festival and expressing hilarity by dolorous croonings (supposed to be songs) interspersed with howls; so we took refuge outside from the noise, under a starlit sky, rendered more beautiful by a fine comet seen by us for the first time. The bedroom at the back of the house was more promising than we had ventured to hope, but the fleas were awful. When I got up in bed during the night, 'pour faire la chasse,' I sprung them in twos and threes, like pheasants in a 'warm corner.'

The church at Ville is worth examination. It has the characteristic Romanesque tower and small spire, and a rich porch with pointed arches, supported on columns of the same date. The entrance door is round-headed, and an ancient font is placed outside by one of the columns. The favourite Guilestre marble is used.

Our attention was attracted early next morning by the sound of many voices singing, and on looking out of the window, we saw a long procession wending its way up the valley. Both sexes took part in it, the men walking first, clad in a sort of white bedgown, girt about the waist, the women following with large white veils thrown over their heads. Banners, maces, and crosses, were carried at intervals, and here and there one or two *curés* walked near them. All chanted a sort of litany as they went, which, at a distance, produced a good effect. The procession must have been more than a quarter of a mile long. Presently another appeared; this, however, was not so numerous, and the vestments were black. Their object was a pilgrimage to the church at Claux, to pray for rain; very little, strange to say, having fallen in that neighbourhood during the summer.

After breakfast we hired a porter to carry some of our provisions, and set off for the Glacier Blanc. I know of few pleasanter walks than

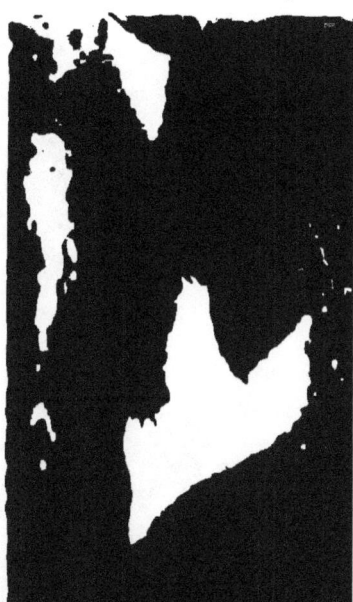

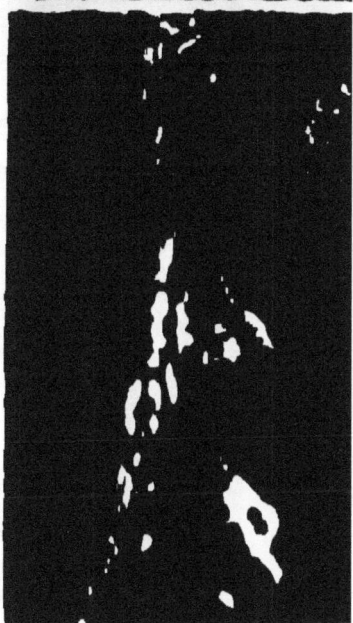

this. The path winds up and down among rocks overgrown with moss and ferns and shaded by trees, the torrent foams below, and the craggy buttresses of the Pelvoux tower in front.[1] From Ville de Vallouise to Claux the valley is thickly peopled and well cultivated, abounding in orchards of apple, cherry, and walnut trees.

At Claux the road crosses the stream from the left to the right bank. Beyond this village the path becomes more rugged, and the scenery wilder. Here and there the rocks are rounded by the pressure of glaciers long since melted away—memorials of the time when the ice streams of the Pelvoux flowed down the Vallouise into the valley of the Durance. At length we arrive on the well-remembered little plain, dotted with plots of rye, oats, potatoes, and cabbages, and watered by a limpid stream, on which stand the châlets of Ailefroide. Turning to the right, we enter the Vallon de St. Pierre, and are at once on new ground. No words can describe the grandeur of this side of the Pelvoux, as it rises precipitously some 7,000 feet above the ravine, crag above crag, and pinnacle above pinnacle, streaked here and there with snow, and wreathed with festoons of broken glacier. At the head of the valley is a small open plain called the Pré de Madame Carle, covered with fragments of stone, among which the beautiful pink granite of the district is conspicuous, and intersected by the many branches of the streams issuing from the glaciers. These it was necessary to cross, in order to gain the right bank of the Glacier Blanc, Mr. Tuckett having failed to reach his *gîte*, for which we were bound, by the other side.

Our porter was not superior to the general law of incapability that distinguishes the natives of these valleys, and lagged far behind, sorely puzzled by the smaller streams. At last he came to the largest, which had given us some trouble ; here he halted, till at last, after much deliberation he converted himself into a Highlander, and cautiously waded across, much to the delight of our guides, who paid him many ironical compliments on his skill and courage.

[1] See a sketch by Mr. Whymper, ' Peaks, Passes, and Glaciers,' second series, vol. ii. p. 236.

C

The contrast between the ends of the Glaciers Blanc and Noir, which almost meet, is very remarkable. The former is a broken cataract of pure white ice, with a blue vaulted terminal cavern; the latter slopes slowly down, dusky with stone and grit, till it buries itself beneath heaps of rubbish. The rounded rocks on the right bank of the Glacier Blanc are easy, though steep, and the views of the Pelvoux,[1] Crête de la Bérarde,[2] and enormous precipices of the Ecrins, are magnificent. Our porter first broke down, and had to be relieved of the greater part of his load; and then, on arriving at the top of the rocks, refused to venture on the ice. This new difficulty, at Mathews's suggestion, was solved by our rushing on to it in a body without paying any attention to him. As his wages were in our pockets he soon followed us, and before long revived under the influence of the cool fresh air. Crossing the glacier, we reached Mr. Tuckett's *gîte*, after about five and a half hours' easy walking. It is a huge mass of rock that has fallen so as to form a sort of tunnel about eight feet by six. We at once set to work, built up the narrow end with stones, spread sods upon the floor, stuffed the crevices with moss and turf to exclude the wind, and soon made quite a luxurious little cabin. The view from the door, of which I have attempted to give some idea,[3] is glorious. It is very nearly the reverse of that seen from Guilestre, and I now began to understand the topography of the Pelvoux group. To the left of the Pelvoux we looked over the Val-louise and the hills on the opposite side of the Durance to the snow-streaked crête of the Pointe des Orches. We had carried some dry juniper wood across the glacier, and found a little more in the neigh-bourhood; so after watching one of the most glorious sunsets that I have ever had the good fortune to behold, we lighted a fire, spread a mac-intosh on the ground, and a plaid over us, and were soon asleep.

We left our *gîte* at 4.35 A.M. on the 26th, and kept to the rocks for

---

[1] Plate I. No. III. is a rough outline of the upper part of the Pelvoux from this spot.
[2] Plate I. No. I.   [3] Plate VI.

: LES ÉCRINS

some time. After we had walked a short distance, the range of the Pelvoux corresponded exactly with the reverse of the outline that I had taken at Guilestre, thus fully confirming the conclusions which I had formed the night before. The Pointe des Ecrins now came into sight,[1] rising from the smooth wide fields of névé that form the upper part of the Glacier Blanc. On this side it is a mass of steep snow, broken here and there into tremendous ice-cliffs and séracs, and terminated by two peaks; one, the highest, a triangle of steep ice divided here and there by ribs, and terminated by two arêtes of broken rock; the other, the lowest, a smooth dome of snow. The middle peak is not visible.

The labyrinth of crevasses seaming the face of the mountain, and the masses of broken ice strewn here and there over the snow, shewed that our task was neither easy nor without danger. After careful examination of the work before us, we determined on trying a slope on the right-hand side, and leaving on our right the ascent to the Col du Glacier Blanc, we advanced up the glacier to the point of attack. Though the snow was in bad order, and the bridges consequently not trustworthy, walking was easy, as the surface of the glacier was in general little broken. On arriving at the foot of the mountain, our work began in earnest; for the next two hours we kept zigzagging up very steep slopes, now and then for a change cutting up an ice wall or walking along a narrow ridge with a steep incline on one side, and a large crevasse on the other. The snow was in the worst possible state, being dry and powdery, covered with a thin frozen crust, and resting in many places on hard ice; thus our work was laborious, and at times a little dangerous.

At last we arrived at the foot of the final peak, and found ourselves cut off from it by a large bergschrund, with the snow bridges in a very rotten condition. This was only narrow enough at one place to give us a chance of crossing, and there a wall of ice had to be scaled and steps cut up a steep slope of snow before the right-hand arête could be reached.

[1] Plate VII. No. I.

c 2

Both the arêtes, instead of rising from the snow, terminated in cliffs some forty feet high.   At last Michel, after carefully scanning the crags, bade us wait a little, and started for the gap that severs the lowest peak from the rest of the mountain, to see whether the rocks could be climbed.   In a few minutes we saw him scrambling up them with evident difficulty, till at last he stood on the arête itself.   We thought the victory was won, and started in pursuit; suddenly he halted, called to us to stop, and turned to descend.   After a long pause he shouted to his brother that he could not come down by the way by which he had ascended, and then began to cut steps towards the narrowest part of the great crevasse.   Jean, after chopping away at the ice for about a quarter of an hour, contrived to worm himself up the wall, and hewed steps upwards to meet him. The labour appeared to be very great, as before a step could be cut, the loose snowy crust had to be dug away until they got to the ice below; the débris came hissing down the slope continually in an incipient avalanche. After about three-quarters of an hour's work, the brothers met, and then cautiously descended to us.   We were glad to see them again, for waiting in the cold, in spite of the fine views of the Meije and of Mont Blanc, was far from pleasant.   Michel's account of the condition of the snow on the arête, combined with his evident doubts as to the prudence of proceeding farther, determined us not to risk the danger of being carried away by an avalanche, so we descended at once.[1]   We could have easily reached the summit of the snow dome in about a quarter of an hour, but as our guides were evidently rather tired with their severe exertions, I did not propose it, expecting that we should have nearly as good a view from the Col des Ecrins below.[2]   I have never ceased to regret this

[1] The wisdom of this course is shewn by the fact that Messrs. Moore, Walker, and Whymper, with Michel Croz, and Christian Almer, in their successful ascent, June 25, 1864, spent 4h. 50' in climbing from the bergschrund to the summit; and 3h. in descending, though the snow was in good order and the weather perfect.

[2] An observation made with my aneroid gave 12,936 feet as the height of the bergschrund. We were thus about 526 feet below the summit, and 128 below the top of the lowest peak.

COL DU GLACIER BLANC.

omission, as the view from that gap is very limited. We cautiously retraced our tracks and found, contrary to our expectations, that the snow had not become any worse; consequently we were able to go for the most part at a good pace, and reached the glacier below in about three-quarters of an hour. Here we halted for lunch, and as soon as hunger was appeased, I set off alone for the Col des Ecrins, which was some seven or eight minutes' walk from us across the glacier. The view greatly disappointed me, but by climbing a little way up some sharp rocks on the right, I got a view down the Vallon de Bonne Pierre to (as I think) the Tête de Loranoure. After a hasty sketch, I set off in pursuit of the others, and soon overtook them. On arriving at the foot of the lateral glacier which descends from the Col du Glacier Blanc, we turned aside, and after an easy climb of rather less than an hour, reached the jagged ridge of rocks on the Col. The view hence is superb, comprising Les Ecrins, the range of the Pelvoux, and part of the valley of the Durance. On the other side we looked over the country near La Grave to the black crags of the Aiguilles d'Arve. Mont Blanc and several of the summits of the Tarentaise ought also to have been visible, but they were hidden by clouds. Thinking that our labours were now nearly over, we spent an hour and a quarter in observing the barometers and sketching. The crags, however, proved more difficult than we had anticipated, and at last, instead of the easy snow slope by which Mr. Tuckett, who discovered the pass, had descended (in July) from the rocks to the upper part of the Glacier des Arsines we found a precipice. We were, therefore, obliged to climb down a very ugly *cheminée*, that cost us much time and trouble. Night was falling fast, and the glacier was at first steep and crevassed. At length, after some little difficulty, we extricated ourselves, and after running over the smoother ice, took to the moraine and succeeded in reaching the pastures just as it became too dark to see objects distinctly. Michel found the narrow track down the valley with wonderful skill; at one place it had been destroyed by the river, and we had to crawl along a steep bank of crumbly soil above the water, frequently upheld by the points of our alpenstocks alone, Michel now and then lighting a match to look for holes for our feet. At length we emerged from the valley upon the *grande route*, passed by Villard d'Arène, walked through several tunnels, and reached the inn at La Grave, after an excursion of eighteen hours. Next morning the effect of the processions was visible in thick clouds and occasional rain, so we were obliged to abandon our intended exploration of the Glacier du Mont de Lans, and drive down to Grenoble, whence we leisurely made our way back to England.

CHAPTER III.

GRANDES ROUSSES—ROAD FROM BOURG D'OISANS TO LA GRAVE—EXCURSION OVER THE GLACIER OF MONT DE LANS—COL DE LA LAUZE—JODRI—DANGEROUS DESCENT—COL DE LA CASSE DÉSERTE—COL DE LA CAVALE—COL DE L'ECHAUDA—MONÊTIER—COL DE BUFFÈRE—COL DES ÉCHELLES DE PLANPINET.

THE result of our journey last year made us anxious to explore thoroughly the range of the Meije, and, if success appeared probable, to attack Les Ecrins again. This time we determined to commence our tour by a short excursion in the neighbourhood of the Grande Chartreuse, and to inaugurate our snow walking by an assault upon the Grandes Rousses,[1] a mountain which, from its isolated position between the Graian and Dauphiné Alps, seemed to promise magnificent views of both, besides having the additional charm of being a virgin summit. Accordingly Messrs. W. and G. S. Mathews, with myself, after a most agreeable excursion in the mountains of the Chartreuse, reached Allevard on the evening of August 3rd, and were joined there by Michel A. Croz and Joseph B. Simond, Jean B. Croz being unfortunately engaged elsewhere. We left Allevard the following afternoon, and walked quietly to La Ferrière, where we slept, *chez* Jourdain, in a plain country auberge. The next morning we had a delightful stroll up to the Sept Laux; thence, on arriving at the col, we turned off to the left, and passing over the ridge by a gap which we propose to call the Col de Billian, descended at once into the valley of the Olle to a châlet called derisively 'La Grande Maison.' Hence we ascended a glen which led

[1] For the details of this excursion, see Mr. W. Mathews's account, 'Alpine Journal,' vol. i. p. 291.

us to the châlet of La Cochette dessus, where we passed a rather uncomfortable night; the accommodation, as is usual where cows are not kept, being on the most limited scale. Leaving at four the next morning, we arrived in less than half an hour at the Col du Couard. Hence we sent on two of our porters with the knapsacks to order a carriage for us at Allemont, and retaining one to carry the theodolite, turned off to the left in the direction of the north peak of the Grandes Rousses, which we had previously reconnoitred from the Col de Billian. A rough climb over broken rocks led us to the glacier, the lower part of which is very steep, so that we had to cut steps in hard ice for a considerable distance, until we got the benefit of a coating of snow. At last we reached the base of a long ridge of rock descending from the northern peak, up which we climbed with some difficulty to the summit of the mountain. Here we saw that the rocks could be approached more easily by getting upon the glacier at a point some distance to the south of the spot where we had first gained the ice, and that the peak was far more accessible on the eastern or Maurienne side, where a fine and comparatively smooth glacier extended up to the very summit.[1] The southern peak appeared also very easy on that side.[2] According to the French engineers, the two peaks are exactly the same height; but W. Mathews's observations give the northern the advantage by about six feet. Though our expectations as regards the view had been raised very high, they had fallen short of the reality. On the north and north-east, indeed, clouds rather obscured the mountains; but we identified the Grande Casse, the Dent Parassée, and the Pourri. Mont Blanc was also visible, his summit appearing from this side unusually flat. To the south, however, there was not a cloud, and a glorious prospect of the Dauphiné Alps lay before us. Plates VIII. and IX. will perhaps give some faint idea of the general effect. On the left (in Plate VIII.)

[1] Plate XIII.

[2] It was ascended by C. Oakley, Esq. last summer (1861). He slept at S. Jean d'Arve, climbed with little difficulty the peak from the Col de Clavans, and returning thither descended to Freney.

is the Crête du Glacier Blanc, above the valley leading to the Col des Arsines.   Then comes the jagged ridge of the Meije with the Glacier de la Meije streaming from it.   Next is the Brèche de la Meije, with its glacier, and through this the double head of the Pelvoux is seen over the Crête de l'Encula, with the Ecrins on its right.   Next is the Râteau, with the long spur running westward, and partly enclosing the head of the Glacier du Mont de Lans.   Over this spur the Ailefroide is seen, and at the end is the Col de la Lauze. Then comes the wide snowfield of the Grand Glacier du Mont de Lans. Peering over it (Plate IX.) are some of the summits south of La Bérarde, and the white peak of the Sommet des Rouies.   Next is the Col de la Muande and the Glacier du Fond, the Cime du Vallon, the Glacier des Sellettes, and the Olan.   The next peak I cannot identify with certainty. The next is probably the Tête de Loranoure, with the Glacier du Pierroux.   Then comes the smooth expanse of the Glacier du Vallon, and the graceful form of the Roche de la Muzelle, the highest peak west of the Vallon de la Muande.   The deep gap to the right is the Col de la Muzelle, and the last peak is probably the Tête de la Muraillette. The ridge of the Grandes Rousses then closes the view.   On the other side of this we looked down the valley of the Olle into that of the Romanche, where the extreme regularity of the fields on the plain at their junction produced a singular effect, making it resemble a piece of green patchwork.   We observed that the Grand Glacier du Mont de Lans was accessible either from the side of La Grave, or, at the western end, by a valley running up towards it from the Romanche.   After spending about two hours most pleasantly on the summit, we again retraced our steps down the arête for above two-thirds of the distance; then turning rather to the left we descended by a steep couloir filled with snow on to the glacier, which we crossed without much trouble, and then climbed down some ice-worn rocks to the little lake of Balme Rousse close to the edge of a precipice.   We were now some distance to the south of and above the Col de Couard; but I believe that our wiser course would have been to have returned thither, and to have followed the path from it to Allemont, which, as we were told at La Cochette, was about an hour and a half's walk from the top of the pass. Instead of this we bore rather to the left, descending the steep side of the mountains by the narrowest of sheep tracks till we reached some alps with châlets. Hence a weary path, undulating up and down the buttresses of the mountain, brought us at last into a small glen, leading into the Combe d'Olle, the left bank of which we followed (at a good height above the stream) for some distance, until at last we descended and crossed to the other side, about a quarter of an hour's walk from Allemont. We found our porters at the *fonderie* just below the village with a carriage in waiting, which in due course conveyed us to Bourg d'Oisans. Trout, fruit, and a hivefull of honey, were welcome luxuries after a couple of days in the mountains, and we did ample justice to the good fare provided for us by the worthy couple at the Hôtel de Milan.

All our endeavours to obtain information at Bourg concerning the valley leading up to the Grand Glacier were fruitless; so we determined to drive to La Grave, where we expected to find a chasseur who knew something of the district. This time we were more fortunate in our weather, and had a lovely afternoon's drive from Bourg to La Grave. On leaving the town the small glaciers of the Tête de la Muraillette and of Villard Eymond are seen among the hills on the south side of the Val de Venéon. Passing through the narrow Gorge des Infernets, from which the Romanche emerges into the cirque of Bourg, the road ascends the steep Rampe des Commères, from which the old Roman road may be seen on the right mounting by sharp zigzags on its way to the pastures of Mont de Lans, where is a ruined arch, said to be Roman. The scenery of all this part of the drive yields in grandeur to none of the other Alpine highways. On reaching the little village of Freney we made further inquiries, and learnt that the highest châlets in the glen running up towards the Grand Glacier were a three hours' walk from Freney, and forty-five minutes from the ice, and were called the Châlets

de la Selle. Shortly after leaving the village we saw the path leading to them; it is nearly sixty-three kilometres from Grenoble, about fifty yards from a wooden bridge over the Romanche. Passing through the village of Le Dauphin, we entered the grand defile of the Combe de Malaval; and just after crossing the limit of the departments of the Isère and Hautes Alpes, had our first view of the offshoots of the great ice-field, streaming into a steep glen, that descended to the Romanche in a series of precipices, down which the glacier torrents fell in cascades. Below are the miserable huts of La Balme, built among and against huge blocks that have tumbled from above. We carefully scanned the cliffs, smoothed and rounded in many places by the extensive ice-streams of past ages, and decided that to all appearance they were inaccessible. Further on, near a little auberge, 'Au Chamois des Alpes,' another offshoot of the glacier is seen on high among the rocks. Soon after we passed the lead mines of Les Freaux, and the beautiful waterfall of La Saute de la Pucelle, and emerged from the barren rocks of the Combe to the pastures and cornfields of La Grave, then reposing under the amber light of the evening sky, while the rich flush of sunset still lingered on the glaciers and crags of the Meije, which were seen by us in unclouded beauty for the first time. The view from the little inn at La Grave is, in my opinion, one of the finest pieces of roadside scenery in the Alps.[1] The jagged pinnacles and smooth precipices of the Meije, and the long crête of the Râteau rise above steep masses of shattered glacier, the torrents from which seam the polished cliffs of protogine. Below, dark shales twisted and riven by the force that burst them asunder and elevated the older rocks five thousand feet above, appear as purple scars among the Alpine pastures which slope down to the turbid waters of the Romanche.

Next morning we crossed the river, and ascended by an excellent path to a group of châlets in a little valley well seen from La Grave, which has been

[1] Plate X.

excavated by the torrents from the glaciers of the Râteau and the west
side of the Meije; these have not only eroded the shale from the western
bank of the valley, but also sawn a deep channel in the crystalline rock.
Crossing the stream, we followed its left bank for a little, then walked
along an old turf-covered moraine, which encloses another, bounding the
heap of rubbish below and over the extremity of the glacier formed by
the ice-streams from the Meije and Râteau. Leaving this natural
causeway, we ascended near a little stream between it and the hill-side;
and then bore up steep slopes, first of turf, and then of broken stone,
varied with a few patches of snow, till we reached a notch in the ridge
(9741 ft., W.M.) which, descending from the western end of the Râteau,
divides the Glacier du Mont de Lans from those in the above valley.
The rock and ice scenery during the whole of the walk through this
miniature Allée Blanche is of the grandest kind, and the western
pinnacle of the Meije is no unworthy rival of the Aiguille du Dru. On
reaching the notch we had a fine view of the Grandes Rousses; the foreground being formed by the snows of the Mont de Lans Glacier. We now
turned upwards, and ascended by the side of the above-named ridge, till
we reached a small patch of black shale forming a kind of island in the
glacier. The col was now plainly visible at the end of a long spur
running westward from the Râteau; between us and it lay a wide
glacier basin, somewhat crevassed; but by a rather circuitous course,
steering first to the left and then to the right, we avoided all difficulties,
and easily reached the snow saddle between the above-named spur
(metamorphic rock) and a little hill of black slate identical with that in
the neighbourhood of La Grave.[1] The latter rises 115 ft. above the col,
and of course commands a more extensive prospect; so we halted
there for some time sketching and luxuriating. The view was superb.

<hr/>

[1] This pass is sometimes termed the Col de
la Selle ('Peaks, Passes, and Glaciers,' 2nd
series, vol. ii. p. 215; Joanne, Itin. Pl. II. p.
168). It is apparently better known in the
district as the Col de la Lauze, and as the
outlier of black slate (Lauze in *patois* = slate)
is so interesting a feature in connexion with
the Col, I prefer to retain it.

Beginning on the east, we had the Ecrins towering grandly above the upper snows of the Glacier de Bonne Pierre; then the higher and lower points of the Crête du Pelvoux, divided by the Crête de la Bérarde, the Ailefroide, the head of the Glacier de la Pilatte, the highest point of the Crête des Bœufs Rouges, the peaks near the Col de Sais, the Sommet des Rouies,[1] looking like an 'expurgated edition of the Ecrins with the objectionable parts omitted,' and the mountains west of the Col de la Muande. As a foreground, there was a dark rugged ridge, striped with snow couloirs and hanging glaciers, forming the opposite boundary of the Vallon de la Selle. On the north lay the peaks of the Grandes Rousses, Mont Blanc, with part of the Pennine chain, and, to the east of these, a number of snowy mountains partially obscured by clouds, among which we identified, with tolerable certainty, the Pourri, the Grande Casse, the Dent Parrassée, and the Glacier de la Vanoise.

Quitting the hill, we walked along the edge of the glacier above the Vallon de la Selle until we gained the summit of a small peak, called on the French map Jodri, near its western end. The view from this point[2] is, of course, nearly the same as that from the Col de la Lauze, except that the greater part of Les Ecrins is concealed by a peak on the other side of the Vallon de la Selle, and the highest summit of the Pelvoux is visible. Hence also we overlooked a part of the glacier draining down to St. Christophe by a rift, called the Brèche de St. Christophe, and also a small plain, dotted with little ponds, beyond which lay the rounded alps of the Mont de Lans, and the peak dividing the Romanche from the Venéon.

From this point we crossed the glacier almost in a straight line, steering rather to the east of the Grandes Rousses; then quitting the ice without difficulty, we traversed a moraine, and descended some very steep and difficult rocks, working gradually to the right, until, after a good deal of awkward scrambling, we found ourselves at the head of the glen that we had observed from La Balme on the previous day.

[1] Plate VII. No. IV.   [2] Plate XI.

Here a thunderstorm, which had for some time been beating up from over La Grave, burst upon us, and ere long drenched us to the skin. Then came a weary descent down débris and rocks, crossing *en route* two or three torrents, one nearly knee deep; then more débris and rocks, often overgrown with grass and brushwood, till we arrived on the brink of a chasm some thirty feet deep, down which rushed a swollen torrent, perhaps twenty feet across. A few yards above, the water fell in a cascade, in the foam of which large stones were bounding like corks; a little further down it disappeared over a rock, whence, as we knew, it fell in a series of leaps to the valley below. Our only way of escape lay over this awkward place; and one by one we crossed it, grasping the rope as a balustrade. Near the opposite side I trod on a loose stone, lost my footing, and remained clinging with one hand to the rope and with one foot fastened down by the stone, till Croz caught me by the collar and hauled me out. My companions got over safely, and thankful at our escape we hurried down a tedious path to the huts of La Balme, reached the high road, and in due course La Grave. This line of descent had been adopted under the guidance of a chasseur of La Grave, named Pic, who has since been termed, not unjustly, the most unblushing liar in Dauphiné. In fine weather it would have been bad enough; in a storm it was little short of madness to attempt it. We ought unquestionably to have descended into the valley leading down to Freney.

We were now anxious to reach the foot of Les Ecrins. Pic informed us that he knew of a spot on the ridge south of the Glacier Blanc, at the head of the Glacier de la Casse Déserte, accessible in six or seven hours from La Grave, where we should find shelter for the night among the rocks, and easily descend on the upper part of the former glacier. Accordingly we started with provisions for two days, and, leaving the high road just beyond the hamlet of Villard d'Arène, kept by the side of the Romanche.

The principal source of this river is the glacier for which we were bound, which lies in a valley between the Roche-Faurio and the Grande

Ruine. Another affluent descends the Vallon de la Cavale, on the other side of the latter mountain. After walking for some time over black shale, we crossed an old moraine of metamorphic rock, and a little farther on arrived at the foot of a wall of the same, up which the path winds steeply; while the Romanche plunges down in a fine cascade. On reaching the top of this we left the path, which ascended further to gain the upland glen leading to the Col des Arsines, and soon reached a grassy meadow by the side of the Romanche. Hence is a fine view of the summits of the Crête du Glacier Blanc.[1] Passing an old mining *baraque*, behind which are four or five moraines arranged opposite to the mouth of our valley, we pushed on rapidly, and, after leaving on our right the glen leading to the Col de la Cavale, in due course arrived at the foot of the glacier. The lower part of this is very easy, and we advanced rapidly till we found ourselves in a kind of amphitheatre, with the steep crags of the Crête du Glacier Blanc on the left, an inaccessible wall of rock in front, and a series of snow slopes on the right, crowned by the splintered pinnacles of La Ruine. We now discovered that, as Croz had from the first predicted, Pic had brought us on a wild-goose chase, and that the whole affair was a delusion. Seeing, however, a col just under the Grande Ruine, we determined to go and look at it. It turned out to be more distant and less accessible than we thought, and a difficult couloir had to be climbed before we arrived at a narrow notch between the Grande Ruine and the Tête de Charrière. Hence is a fine view of Les Ecrins,[2] and of the range of the Pelvoux, over which a storm was beating up towards us. As the afternoon was far advanced, the weather threatening, and one part of the descent looked very dubious, we thought it better to return to La Grave. Our return by the couloir required great caution, but once off that we had no further trouble, and by quick walking regained the *baraque* at dusk. My companions halted here to refresh, but having a lively recollection of my night walk of the year before, I

[1] Plate V. No. I.   [2] Plate VII. No. II.

pushed on with Simond and reached La Grave at 9.40 P.M.   The rest
of the party came in three-quarters of an hour later, having lost their
way in the dark.

In consequence of this failure, we determined to go to La Bérarde by the
Col de la Cavale, and so complete the exploration of the range of the Meije.
We followed the now familiar road until we came to the junction of the
glacier streams, when we turned aside to the right.   After walking up
the débris-strewn bed of the valley, we reached the foot of the glacier,
which descends from the col on the west and the spur of the Grande
Ruine on the south.   On the north are cliffs, over which appears the
end of a small glacier.   The position of the col is obvious, at the lowest
point of the ridge;[1] but the upper part of the glacier is steep and broken,
so that care is requisite at times.   The snow reaches to within a few feet
of the top of the pass, a shattered ridge of protogine rock split into
great square blocks.   Hence is a grand view of the Meije, which does
not look more promising on this side than on the other.   To the left of
this is seen the chain dividing the Vallon de la Selle from the Vallon des
Etançons, the peaks near St. Christophe, east and west of the Vallon
de la Muande, and, closing the view, the pinnacles of the Grande Ruine.
Looking back, we see the mountains near the Col de Lautaret and
above Briançon.

On the western side of the pass a precipitous cliff leads down to a
steep snow couloir, which gradually expands into a short smooth glacier.
After quitting this, we descended sometimes by climbing down rocks,
sometimes by sliding in small avalanches of pebbles down long slopes of
débris, until, when within a few hundred feet of the bottom of the valley,
a precipice brought us suddenly to a stop, and obliged us to reascend
slightly and work to the left, till we found a practicable line of descent.
The view of the Meije and the Glacier des Etançons from the bottom of
the valley induced us to halt for a sketch;[2] after which we walked on for

[1] Plate V. No. IV.

[2] Plate XII.   The gap on the left of the Meije is the Brèche, which is obviously accessible on the side.

some distance, then crossed to the right bank of the stream, and in due
course arrived at La Bérarde. We saw *en route* the Col de la Casse
Déserte, the descent from which appeared practicable, though difficult.
The Rodiers received us hospitably, but we did not stay much in doors,
for the evening was one of the most lovely that I have ever seen, even
in the Alps, and we lay stretched upon our plaids on the grassy hillocks,
watching the rosy tints of sunset fading through every gradation of
colour into the tender purples of a summer's night, while star after star
shone out in the darkening sky.

Starting from La Bérarde on a lovely morning, we walked up the
valley towards the Glacier de la Pilatte, and in about an hour arrived at
a little plain opposite to the opening of the glen leading to the Glacier
du Chardon. . This commands a glorious view of the Ailefroide, and
would be an excellent site for a mountain inn. On reaching the foot of
the Glacier de la Pilatte, we ascended the right moraine for some distance;
and then, after crossing the ice, climbed some easy rocks on the left bank.
Hence is a fine view of Les Ecrins, the three summits being visible.[1]
Returning to the glacier, we took a wide circuit under the cliffs of the
Crête des Bœufs Rouges, in order to avoid the séracs in the middle, and at
last, after mounting some steep slopes of snow, arrived at the foot of
a wall of rock formed by a spur of the Ailefroide. Mr. Tuckett, the
discoverer of the pass, found this comparatively easy; such was not our
experience, the difference being no doubt due to the melting of the snow
in the couloirs. On gaining the top of the cliff we stepped upon the edge
of a snowfield sloping down to the Glacier du Sélé. The view of the basin
of the Glacier de la Pilatte, of the ice stream from the Col de Sais, and a
tributary on the west of it, and of the Sommet des Rouies, is very
striking. A spur of the Ailefroide, terminating in a low peak,[2] is just on
the left of the pass, and the scenery of the whole chain, from that mountain to the Pelvoux, which remains in sight during the first part of the

[1] Plate VII. No. III.   [2] Plate I. No. IV.

D

descent, can hardly be surpassed. We again took a circuitous course, keeping first near the right bank of the glacier, then crossing over to the left to avoid the crevasses in the middle.   Lower down the ice stream became so much broken that we were obliged to quit it for the moraine, and on leaving this we descended some steep cliffs, not without a few *mauvais pas*. To these succeeded a long slope of shingle, a *spécialité* of Dauphiné very trying both to the legs and to the temper. Most welcome was the comparatively level ground at the head of the Combe de Sapenière, by which we reached the châlets of Ailefroide, and, in due course, Ville de Vallouise.

The fleas were as vigorous as ever, and murdered sleep so effectually that, finding the weather next morning very unsettled and ourselves rather tired, we determined to abandon Les Ecrins, and go to Monêtier to rest.   Retracing our steps to Claux, we followed a well-marked mule track to the summit of the Col de l'Echauda, and then descended through Alpine pastures to the little town.   The Pelvoux is a grand object during the first part of the ascent, and the Glaciers of Monêtier and Prés les Fonds are seen during the descent.   A pass to the foot of the Glacier Blanc might perhaps be made over the former of these.   Monêtier, with its natural warm baths, its comfortable Hôtel de l'Europe (*chez* Arnaud), its picturesque views of the above glaciers,[1] and the Rochebrune towering over the forts of Briançon, is a pleasant halting place for a day or two.   We however left it next morning, and walked up to the Col de Buffère; from which we descended through exquisite scenery of alp, and cliff, and forest, into the Val Clairée; where, about a mile above the village of Neuvache, we passed some of the most magnificent domes of ice-worn rock that I have ever seen.   Later in the day we crossed into Piedmont by the slippery steps of Les Échelles de Planpinet, and halted for the night at the busy village of Bardonnèche.

[1] Plate V. No. II.

CHAPTER IV.

JOURNEY OF 1864.

THE AIGUILLES D'ARVE AND THE COL DE GOLÉON—LA GRAVE—EXCURSION TO GLACIER OF
MONT DE LANS—FRENEY—COL DE VENOS—EXCURSION UP VALLON DE LA SELLE—COL
DE LA MUANDE—VAL GODEMAR—CORPS—LA MURE—LAFFREY—DESCENT TO GRENOBLE.

OUR expeditions had still left one corner of Dauphiné unexamined, the
neighbourhood of the Col de la Muande, and I was therefore not quite
positive about the identity of all the peaks south of the Venéon.   This
made me anxious to conclude my visit to the Alps by crossing from the
Maurienne by the Aiguilles d'Arve, intersecting the *massif* surrounding
the Venéon from north to south, and descending either by the Val
Godemar or Jouffrey.   My companion, Mr. R. W. Taylor, kindly yielded
to my desire, and submitted to the prospect of scanty dinners and
abundant fleas with praiseworthy resignation.   We brought Joseph B.
Simond with us from Chamouni, where we had met Messrs. Moore
and Whymper returning from their successful campaign.[1]   After spending several days in exploring the country between Courmayeur and the
head of the valley of the Arc, we reached St. Michel on the evening of
July 18.   A short distance to the west of this town a valley runs up
into the range dividing the Maurienne from Dauphiné, from the head
of which two passes lead to La Grave by the high road over the Col du

---

[1] Messrs. Moore, Walker, and Whymper,
accompanied by Michel A. Croz and Christian Almer, after some explorations in the
neighbourhood of the Aiguilles d'Arve,
crossed the Brèche de la Meije from La

Grave to La Bérarde (June 23), ascended
Les Ecrins from the Col des Ecrins (June 25),
and made a new pass from the head of the
Vallon des Bancs to the Glacier de la Pilatte
(June 27).

Lantaret. The higher, called the Col du Galibier, comes down at the Hospice on the top of the pass; the lower, the Col de Goléon, close to La Grave. We chose the latter, not only as being a more direct route, but also as going nearer to the Aiguilles d'Arve.

The above-mentioned valley is called Valloire, which name is also borne by the principal village; the shortest road to this from St. Michel is across a shoulder of the mountains south of that town. Leaving St. Michel at 5.30 on a cloudy morning, we followed a good mule path, first through gardens and cultivated fields, then through woods and pastures, up to a grassy col, on which stand a cross and a small chapel. About a mile from St. Michel the road divides; had it not been for the postman to Valloire, we should have gone wrong by keeping straight on, instead of turning to the right. The col, as we were told, commands a view of the Aiguilles d'Arve, but they were then veiled in clouds. The scene, however, in front of us was very pretty; the mountains were pyramidal in form, and covered with pastures and woods; several groups of châlets and villages were dotted about; two of which, high on the opposite hill-side, with bright white cottages, looked wonderfully clean and snug after the dark stone hovels to which we had of late been accustomed. In the bottom of the valley, a little above Valloire, were some curious projecting ridges of rock. From the col a sloping path led us down through one or two small hamlets to Valloire, from which rather more than an hour's walk brought us to the scattered village of Bonnenuit. We halted at the auberge (one of the highest houses in the place) for some lunch. It was but one degree above a châlet, and the bill of fare comprised little beyond bread, cheese, honey, and an omelette. It commands a good view of the two highest peaks of the Aiguilles d'Arve, and a careful examination convinced me that Croz was in the right in his advice, given me in the most paternal manner at Chamouni: 'As for the Aiguilles d'Arve, M. Bonney, I recommend you to leave them for somebody else.' They are about as uninviting a pair as I have ever seen—equally black, craggy, and forbidding on all sides.

About a mile after leaving Bonnenuit we crossed from the right to the left bank of the stream, and then followed a path leading into a lateral valley. This, after crossing one rivulet, turns up the glen drained by the next, no great distance from some scattered châlets. This glen leads right up to the Col de Goléon, the lowest point in a long ridge of shaly rock, the strata of which are highly inclined and much twisted; just on the right of it is a blunt triangular point. Throughout the ascent, on looking back, a fine craggy peak (the Aiguille Noir?) is seen across the valley opposite to the mouth of the glen, a little to the right, and after a while a flat-topped snow mountain (Mont Tabor?) appears on the right of this. Just before reaching the col we had a glimpse of the Rochebrune and some of the hills above Briançon. On reaching the summit of the pass a magnificent view burst upon us. Directly opposite to us rose the Meije, thrusting out a long jagged spur to the left, which overhung the snowfields of a glacier (de l'Homme?), separated by a lower ridge from the Glacier de la Meije. One peak (probably the Pic Signalé of the map) rose far above the rest of the spur. Beyond the Meije was the Râteau; and beyond was the spur from it to the Col de la Selle, and the whole extent of the great glacier. The sky was covered with clouds, but happily they only just caught the summits. Immediately below us a steep descent led down into a flat basin, at the head of which was a glacier. Around this lay four peaks; the one on the other bank of the glacier had a snow slope on its right side, and a stone man on the summit. Just at the head of the glacier were two summits, that on the left a snow dome, the other and higher chiefly of rock; and, still further to the right, was a rocky peak, rising in a smooth slope from the glacier. I think that the 'Stone Man' peak on the left is the one usually termed Aiguille de Goléon. On reaching the valley below, I saw that an arm of the glacier led up under the rocky peak on the right to a sort of col, apparently very near to the highest summit of the Aiguilles d'Arve; which, however, appear to stand quite to the north of the watershed between Dauphiné and the Maurienne. The wind blew bitterly over the pass, but it was impossible to leave such a scene unsketched, so I worked away for nearly an hour and obtained a record of the whole range. I had hardly finished before the clouds dropped again on the Meije and blotted out the view. Then, after a hasty memorandum of the glacier at the head of the valley, I rushed down the steep shaly descent in order to restore circulation, and joined my companions, who were waiting for me in shelter below. The head of the valley into which we descended is a flat swampy plain, traversed by streamlets from the glacier. Crossing these we gained the right bank, obtaining on the way another view of the double-headed Aiguilles d'Arve, rising behind the ridge enclosing the glacier. A rough track round the base of the Goléon brought us down to another grassy plain, on which stood several châlets. Passing through these we descended a tortuous path among the fields to the further end of the tunnel, just east of La Grave, by the right bank of the gorge. I believe that we should have gained time had we crossed the stream at the above-mentioned plain, and followed its left bank, since we should thus have avoided the sinuosities of the path.

We met with a hearty welcome at La Grave, and were favoured with a call in the course of the evening from our friend Pic, who volunteered several remarkable topographical statements to shew that his talent for mendacity had not been suffered to lie idle since my last visit. Next morning we started for the Col de la Lauze, intending to cross it and descend to St. Christophe. There was a lovely sunrise, but clouds soon gathered, and before we reached the well-known gap, snow fell heavily. After waiting for nearly an hour, we took advantage of a brief gleam, and gained the glacier. The snow before long fell thicker than ever; so, after advancing some distance further, we saw that even if we succeeded in finding the way there was no hope of any view from the col. We therefore descended to La Grave, and drove down to Freney, intending, if the weather became more promising, to walk up to the Châlets de la Selle, and try the pass from that side. The rain, however, fell heavily, so that we abandoned our purpose, and drove on to Freney. The even-

ing, however, turned out much finer than we had ventured to hope, and we strolled some distance down towards the Rampe des Commères. Here we accidentally met M. Martin, of the Hôtel de Milan at Bourg, who appeared really delighted to see us again, and greeted us most warmly.

The next morning we set off in a thick mist for the Col de Venos. A steep ascent over rough ground brought us to the little village of Mont de Lans; thence the path turns to the right, just at the outside of the village, and runs for some distance in that direction, slightly descending. Bearing then up the hill-side to the left, it enters a little valley and ascends by the side of a small stream. The mist still lay thick around, and we began to fear that we should see nothing, when, just on reaching the stretch of pasture land forming the upper part of the pass, we suddenly caught a glimpse of the sun; in a few minutes more the veil of vapour parted in the middle and fell back into the valley on either side. A faint haze filled the air, through which the mountains gleamed in the morning light with a delicate softness that no description can render. Steep grassy hills, overgrown with wild flowers, enclose the marshy plain on the summit of the pass, commanding, of course, a more extended prospect. We ascended two or three hundred feet up one of these (on the right), and then sat down to enjoy the view. Behind us, on the opposite side of the Romanche, the Grandes Rousses rose above the clouds, shewing the northern and southern peaks with the glacier covering their eastern flank.[1] Before us was the beautiful Roche de la Muzelle,[2] the smooth expanse of the Glacier du Vallon, and the group of peaks immediately on the west of the Vallon de la Muande. Then came a fine view of the range forming the eastern boundary of the same valley,[3] and to the left of this a corner of the

[1] Plate XIII. (1) southern peak, (2) northern peak.
[2] Plate IX. (10.) This peak is seen from the upper part of the Combe d'Olle.
[3] Namely, the Tête du Cronzel, the Tête des Fétoules, and the Tête de l'Être, with the triangular peak of the Sommet des Rouies seen over the ridge joining it to the last named.

Ailefroide projected beyond the hills cutting us off from the glacier of Mont de Lans.

After spending an hour and a quarter in admiring and sketching the view, we descended by a steep zigzag path to Venos, and turned into old Paquet's auberge. Changes had taken place since last we saw it; Madame Paquet had died the year after our visit, and the then *fille* had been promoted to the vacant place. The auberge also had been enlarged; there were now three clean comfortable single-bedded rooms, and one good chamber containing four beds. Old Paquet shewed us over his improvements, of which he evidently was justly proud.

We walked thence through the wild scenery of the Clapier de St. Christophe to that village, where also we found improvements. The auberge has been rebuilt, and now contains a very tolerable *salle*, and at least two comfortable beds. The afternoon was still young, so I walked up the Vallon de la Selle in order to make amends, as far as possible, for our failure of the day before. Taylor followed the road towards Les Étages, being anxious to get a view of Les Ecrins. Mounting the rising ground above the village, on the left bank of the gorge of the Torrent du Diable, I gained the opening of the Vallon de la Selle, and crossed the stream by a bridge. Little can be seen of the Glacier du Mont de Lans, but the precipices supporting it are very grand. Before long the Glacier de la Selle appears, with the serrate ridge on its left bank. In about an hour, after crossing a dirty stream which falls down the cliffs below the Glacier du Mont de Lans, I reached a châlet, the owner of which hospitably asked me to stay and refresh myself. I promised to do so on my return, and walked on a little farther, until I got a good view of the head of the valley. After sketching it, I went back to the châlet and was regaled with *brousse*, for which all offers of payment were positively refused. I was informed that a path to Freney led up the cliffs just behind the châlet, which went on the west of the Glacier du Mont de Lans. This is doubtless the pass which was pointed out to me from the top of Jodri the previous year. I did not see the Col de la Lauze itself;

it was concealed by part of the right bank of the valley. The mountains of St. Christophe, the Glacier du Fond, and the Cime du Vallon, glowing in the evening light, lay before me as I descended.

We could not find any one at St. Christophe who knew the Col de la Muande, so we engaged a man to carry our knapsacks to the top of the pass, and determined to take the chance of picking up some information at the higher châlets. Accordingly we started, rather later than we ought, on a lovely morning, and followed the road to La Bérarde as far as the division of the valleys.

A rough path leads down to the level of the torrent draining the Vallon de la Muande, and crosses by a bridge to the left bank. Some brushwood and a few stunted trees grow near the mouth of the valley; after that it is little better than a barren waste. A few meadows surround the huts of La Lavey, where we managed to obtain some general directions about the course to be taken, and on leaving we crossed back to the right bank of the stream. From this hamlet the col is seen above the Glacier des Fonds, immediately under a craggy buttress of the Sommet des Rouies, with a blunt point of rock just on the right. Still farther to the right are the black cliffs of the Cime du Vallon dividing the Glacier des Sellettes from the above-mentioned glacier. A somewhat tedious walk through a wilderness of stones brought us to the foot of a steep slope of loose moraine, up which we scrambled and found ourselves on a tolerably level plateau of ice sprinkled over with stones. We now halted a moment to reconnoitre. The upper part of the glacier before us was obviously easy; the lower as obviously difficult. Two routes appeared practicable; one was to climb a steep and very broken icefall, just in front, under the cliffs on the right bank of the glacier, the other to cross nearly to the left bank and mount by a long slope running diagonally right across the glacier. This, though very circuitous and not without difficulty, appeared the more feasible; Simond, however, after carefully scanning the labyrinth before us, pronounced it 'pas trop mauvais,' and advanced to the attack. More than hour was spent in hewing steps up steep slopes of hard ice, among a maze of crevasses, the excitement of which was heightened by the consciousness that we were within the range of stones from the cliffs, showers of which were obviously far from uncommon.   At last new snow began to encrust the ice, the ascent to become more gentle, and the crevasses less frequent ; though here and there one had to be passed, which, in a worse state of the snow, would have been troublesome.   The actual col is on the snow-field, but a descent of a few feet leads to a natural gateway in the cliff, some thirty feet wide, separated by a short interval of rock from a steep snow couloir, that gradually widens out into a short level glacier, beyond which we looked down into the Val Godemar, on the other side of which rose a long dark precipitous ridge, streaked with snow couloirs and hanging glaciers, and divided by a well-marked depression into two summits, whereof that on the right was the higher.   On the left were the cliffs of the Sommet des Rouies; on the right the Olan and its neigh-bours.   Behind, we looked back to the Grandes Rousses and the lower mountains near Bourg d'Oisans.   After dismissing our porter, who refused to accompany us further, we descended on to the glacier, making for a moraine at its extremity on the right.   Here we saw that we should have no great difficulty in reaching some tracks which were visible below. Accordingly we descended a steep slope of loose stones, followed by turf banks and rocks, bearing at first rather to the right and then working to the left, so as to reach an alp, the path over which brought us in a few minutes to a solitary châlet, tenanted by a *berger* from Provence, who lived there all alone tending 600 sheep.   Here we halted to sketch a fine mountain to the south of the Col du Célar.[1]   A curious needle-like pinnacle of rock to the west of us also attracted our attention.   A steep descent now led us down to the hamlet of Riou du Sap, by the yellow waters of the Severnisse, after crossing which we reached, in rather less than half an hour, La Chapelle (auberge, *chez* Armand) just in time to escape a thunderstorm.

[1] Plate L No. II.   Perhaps the Pic Bonvoisin, E. M. F.   Mont Garroux, of Bourcet.

The inhabitants were very curious as to our object in travelling; even the *maire* cross-examined us; evidently they thought that mines were the real attraction, for pleasure and health seemed such inadequate motives; until it suddenly struck one of them that the mountain air was fresher than that of the valleys, when the explanation was at once accepted. They, however, and the goodwife of the house, were all very civil. We had a really good dinner of trout and chamois, beds in a neighbouring house, unhappily swarming with fleas, and a most moderate bill on our departure.

We had hoped that our expedition would have allowed us to see something of the range between the Col de la Muande and the Col de Sais, so that we might have reconnoitred the ascent to a pass on the east of the Sommet des Rouies, the northern side of which is probably practicable. In this we had been disappointed, as a buttress of rock had entirely obstructed our view in that direction, and all that we could infer from the general character of the country was that it would be very difficult to find the road without some preliminary exploration. Moreover La Chapelle, to which the state of the provision bag had obliged us to descend, is rather too far down the valley for the starting point in a new excursion. Accordingly, as our time was running short, and we both felt the want of nourishing diet and sound sleep, we determined neither to attempt to recross the range nor to penetrate into the Val Jouffrey, an expedition which would have required a very long day's walk in order to reach decent quarters. The unsettled state of the weather also helped to deter us from plunging again into the mountains; so quitting La Chapelle next morning, we walked along a very fair char road down the Val Godemar. The cliffs about the Col du Célar must be fine, but the clouds only allowed us to have glimpses of them. The scenery of the valley is not remarkable, but a fine range of precipices on the other side of the Drac is visible for the greater part of the descent.

After a brief halt at St. Firmin, a considerable village near the mouth

of the Val Godemar, we pushed on and gained the high road in the valley
of the Drac, by which we reached the busy little town of Corps in rather
more than an hour's walking. The road rises gradually as it approaches
this place in order to avoid a gorge, and runs along the flanks of steep
hills of highly inclined and contorted strata of shaly clay and limestone. .
The Drac valley, though barren at places, is rather pretty, and some of
the views up it from near Corps are striking. It seems to widen, and
the hills on each side to become lower, as its head is approached; so that
any one ignorant of the direction of its stream would suppose its course
to be southward.

Corps is the place of departure for the notorious La Sallette, which
is distant about two hours' journey among the mountains. After a
long delay in starting, we were forwarded in a semi-public conveyance,
containing, besides ourselves, two priests and two women, pilgrims from
La Sallette. They had travelled continuously for four days to reach the
spot, and after a few hours' stay were returning, bearing with them
water from the miraculous spring, and various books of devotion, as
souvenirs. The scenery of the Drac valley improves after leaving Corps;
the road ascends gradually, and at last turns away from the river; then
descending into a ravine, in which are some curious rock pinnacles, it
crosses the Bonne, and winds tortuously up to the little town of La
Mure. Beyond this place the road, still rising gradually, passes in
succession the Lac de Pierre-Châtel, the Lac de Petit-Chat, and the
Grand Lac de Laffrey. These are all very pretty. Looking one way, the
mountains near the Drac are seen to rise as a background; looking the
other, those of the Chartreuse district. A slight ascent leads to Laffrey,
a poor village of little more than a single street; but in a wall on the
left near the church is a stone that marks the spot where Napoleon on
his return from Elba met the troops of Marchand, sent from Grenoble to
arrest him.

Soon afterwards we gained the edge of the plateau, and looked down
into the basin of the Romanche upon a scene not easily forgotten. It was

evening, and the cloudless sky glowed with amber light ; far below lay the shady depths of the Combe de Gavet, overhung by the crags of the Belledonne, and backed up by a snowy peak of the Grandes Rousses, 'lying sunset flushed.' At our feet were spread the green meadows of Vizille, the rich fields climbing up the hills behind the town; the Romanche, gleaming as it rolled down towards Grenoble; and beyond these rose the beautiful outlines of the limestone summits of the Chartreuse.

A steep descent led us into Vizille, whence in due course we arrived at Grenoble, not sorry to find ourselves once more among the comforts of civilisation, and well able to appreciate the hearty welcome and attentions of the host and hostess of the Hôtel de l'Europe.

APPENDIX.

THE great difficulty to the ordinary tourist in Dauphiné is the bad accommodation so universal in the country. I therefore venture to suggest a few days' excursions which may be made without inconvenience, even by ladies who are good walkers:—

1. Grenoble to Bourg d'Oisans (carriage).
2. Visit the Granges of Huez, or some other point of view on the north side of the Romanche valley.
3. To St. Christophe; excursion up the Vallon de la Selle.
4. By La Bérarde to the foot of the Ailefroide, returning to Venos.
5. Over the Col de Venos to Frenoy; there be met by a carriage from Bourg, and drive to La Grave.
6. Excursion to the Col de Goléon, or to some point on the north side of the valley of Romanche.
7. Excursion to the Col de la Lauze.
8. Drive over the Col du Lautaret to Briançon, or walk over the Col des Arsines (much finer) to Monêtier; thence drive to Briançon.

From Briançon the traveller can go over the Genèvre to Susa, or descend the valley of the Durance, either to Guilestre whence he can visit the Viso, or to Embrun whence he can go southward. I have omitted from this tour the eastern side of the Pelvoux, because at present there is no sleeping place fit for a lady in the Vallouise. The only plan would be to drive from Briançon to Ville de Vallouise, and walk thence either to the foot of the Glacier Blanc, or as far in that direction as time allowed, returning the same night to Briançon, or going on to Guilestre. This would involve a long day of at least sixteen hours.

Some of the finest scenery of Dauphiné, as may have been gathered from my accounts, can be seen from the high road between Grenoble and Briançon. I most strongly recommend this course to travellers going to or coming from Turin. It takes a day or so longer than the Cenis, but is incomparably finer. Leaving Paris by the night express, Grenoble is reached about 11 A.M., and Bourg d'Oisans may be gained without difficulty by 8 that evening. Briançon can be reached the next night, and Turin the third. If more time can be devoted to the journey, there is a first-rate hotel at Grenoble, and very fair accommodation at Bourg, La Grave, Monêtier, and Briançon, especially at the first place. There are diligences along the road.

I may also indicate a high level tour for the Alpine climber, starting from Bourg d'Oisans:—

1. To the Chälets de la Selle above Freney.
2. Ascend Jodri, follow the Glacier du Mont de Lans to the Col de la Lauze, and descend to La Grave.
3. By Col de la Cavale to La Bérarde.
4. By Col du Sélé to Chälets of Ailefroide.
5. By Col du Glacier Blanc to La Grave or Monétier.

This may be rendered less laborious by the following alteration:—

4. By Col du Sélé to Ville de Vallouise.
5. To Gîte by the side of Glacier Blanc.
6. By Col du Glacier Blanc to La Grave or Monétier.

If this tour be too long, I should advise: Arrange to visit the country from the Maurienne. Cross the Col de Goléon to La Grave, then the Col de la Cavale, the Col du Sélé, and the Col du Glacier Blanc. These four passes will give the traveller a very clear idea of the grandest and most important parts of the district.

Guides.—So far as I know them, the few to be found in the country are of little or no value; sometimes, indeed, worse than useless. The following foreign guides can be recommended. (I give the dates of their excursions):—

Michel Auguste Croz, La Tour, Chamouni, 1860, 1862 (twice), 1863, 1864.

Jean Baptiste Croz, La Tour, Chamouni, 1862.

Joseph Basil Simond, Argentière, 1863, 1864.

Peter Perrn, Zermatt, 1862.

Christian Almor, Grindelwald, 1864.

Guide Books and other sources of information:—

'Joanne, Itinéraire Descriptif et Historique du Dauphiné.' 2 vols. Paris: Hachette and Co. An excellent work; the second volume chiefly refers to the district which I have described.

'The Alpine Guide: Western Alps.' (Longmans.)

'An Excursion in Dauphiné,' by Principal Forbes, affixed to 'Norway and its Glaciers.' A. and C. Black, Edinburgh.

'Peaks, Passes, and Glaciers,' second series, vol. ii. (Longmans) contains:—'The Col de la Tempe,' by R. C. Nichols, F.S.A. 'The Val de St. Christophe and the Col de Sais,' by T. G. Bonney, M.A., F.G.S. 'Sketch of the Col de la Selle (de la Lauze),' by F. C. Blackstone, B.C.L., F.R.G.S. 'The Ascent of Mont Pelvoux,' by E. Whymper.

'The Alpine Journal,' vol. i. (Longmans) contains:—No. 2. 'An Excursion in Dauphiné,' by T. G. Bonney, M.A., F.G.S. No. 4. 'Explorations in the Alps of Dauphiné during July, 1862,' by F. F. Tuckett, F.R.G.S. No. 6. 'The Grandes Rousses of Dauphiné,' by W. Mathews jun., M.A., F.G.S.; 'The Range of the Meije,' by T. G. Bonney, M.A., F.G.S.

A list of other works, referring more or less directly to Dauphiné, will be found given in 'The Alpine Guide.'

ITINERARY.

Note.—The times given are exclusive of halts. Our rate of walking is, I believe, generally rather above than below the average. .

1860. —Aug. 10. Bourg d'Oisans to Venos, 2h. 30'. Thence to St. Christophe, 2h. 30'. Total, 5h.

Aug. 11. St. Christophe to La Bérarde, 3h.

Aug. 12. La Bérarde to Col de Sais, about 4h. 30'. Descent, about 2h. 30'. Total 7h.

Aug. 13. La Bérarde to Bourg d'Oisans, about 7h.

Aug. 15. La Bessée to Ville de Vallouise, 1h. 30'. Thence to Châlets of Ailefroide, 2h. 20'. Thence to Gîte on Pelvoux, 1h. 40'. Total, 5h. 30'.

Aug. 17. Partial ascent of Pelvoux, 3h. 30'. Descent to valley, 2h. 30'. Thence to Ville, 2h. Thence to La Bessée, 1h. 30'. Total, 9h. 30'.

1862.—Aug. 23. La Chianale to Col de Maurin, 2h. 8'. Thence to Col de Cristillan, 2h. 20'. Thence to Ceillac, 2h. 20'. Thence to the high road to Guilestre, 1h. 25'. Thence to Guilestre, 1h. Total, 9h. 13'.

Aug. 25. Ville de Vallouise to foot of Glacier Blanc, 3h. 30'. Thence to Gîte, 1h. 55'. Total, 5h. 25'.

Aug. 26. Gîte to foot of Les Ecrins, 2h. 25'. Thence to crevasse at foot of peak, 2h. 5'. Descent of mountain, 45'. Thence to lateral glacier, from Col du Glacier Blanc, 1h. Ascent to Col, 52'. Descent to moraine of Glacier des Arsines, 2h. 20'. Thence to La Grave, 3h. 30'. Total, 12h. 57'.

1863.—Aug. 5. Allevard to La Ferrière, 2h. 5'.

Aug. 6. La Ferrière to Col des Sept Laux, 4h. 30'. Thence to Col de Billian, 1h. 5'. Thence to La Grande Maison, 1h. 50'. Thence to Châlet of Cochette Dessus, 1h. 18'. Total, 8h. 43'.

Aug. 7. La Cochette to Col du Couard, 25'. Thence to foot of arête of Grandes Rousses, 3h. Ascent to summit, 1h. 37'. Descent to end of Glacier, 2h. 35'. Thence to Lac de Balme Rousse, 43'. Thence to Allemont, 3h. 15'. Total, 11h. 35'.

Aug. 8. La Grave to cleft in rocky ridge, 3h. 35'. Thence to Col de la Lauze, 1h. 43'. Col to Jodri, 1h. 17'. Thence to end of glacier, 42'. Descent to La Balme, 2h. 40'. Total, 9h. 57'.

Aug. 10. La Grave to Baraque, 2h. 33'. Thence to Glacier de la Casse Déserte, 45'. Thence to Col, 4h. 7'. Descent of couloir, 50'. Thence to Baraque, 2h. 33'. Thence to La Grave, 2h. Total, 12h. 48'.

Aug. 12. La Grave to entrance of Vallon de la Cavale, 2h. 47'. Thence to Col, 2h. 45'. Descent to Vallon des Etançons, 2h. 10'. Thence to La Bérarde, 1h. Total, 8h. 42'.

Aug. 13. La Bérarde to foot of Glacier de la Pilatte, 1h. 55'. Thence to foot of wall of rock, 2h. 50'. Ascent to Col du Sélé, 40'. Descent to side of

E

glacier, 1h. 10'. Thence to Châlets of Ailefroide, 1h. 7'. Thence to Ville de Vallouise, 1h. 15'. Total, 8h. 57'.

Aug. 14. Ville to Col de l'Echauda, 3h. 30'. Thence to Monêtier, 1h. 25'. Total, 4h. 55'.

Aug. 15. Monêtier to Col de Buffère, 2h. 5'. Thence to Neuvache, 1h. 42'. Thence to Col des Echelles, 1h. 20'. Thence to Bardonnèche, 1h. 10'. Total, 6h. 17'.

1861.—July 18. St. Michel to Valloire, 2h. 20'. Thence to Bonnenuit, 1h. 10'. Thence to Col de Goléon, 2h. 50'. Thence to La Grave, 2h. 15'. Total, 8h. 35'.

July 19. La Grave to point on Glacier du Mont de Lans, 3h. 20'. Descent to La Grave, 1h. 55'. Total, 5h. 15'.

July 20. Freney to Col du Venos, 2h. Thence to Venos, 50'. Thence to St. Christophe, 1h. 55'. Excursion in Vallon de la Selle, 2h. Total, 6h. 45'.

July 21. St. Christophe to La Lavey, 2h. 15'. Thence to Col de la Muande, 4h. 10'. Descent of couloir and glacier, 25'. Thence to Riou du Sap, 1h. 35'. Thence to La Chapelle, 1h. 15'. Total, 9h. 40'.

July 22. La Chapelle to St. Firmin, 2h. 45'. Thence to Corps, 1h. 45'. Total, 4h. 30'.

TABLE OF HEIGHTS.

Authorities. — E. M. F. = État-Major Français.   F. F. T. = F. F. Tuckett.
W. M. = W. Mathews jun.   T. G. B. = T. G. Bonney.

Name	Height in feet	Authority	Method
PEAKS			
Pointe des Ecrins :—			
East Peak .	13,462	E. M. F.	△
Centre Peak .	13,396	,,	,,
North-West Peak	13,058	,,	,,
La Meije .	13,081	,,	,,
Grand Pelvoux :—			
Highest Peak .	12,973	F. F. T.	Bar.
Pic de la Pyramide .	12,920	E. M. F.	△
L'Ailefroide .	12,873	,,	,,
Crête du Pelvoux :—			
East Peak .	12,845	,,	,,
West Peak .	11,772?	,,	,,
Crête de l'Encula .	12,399	,,	,,
Le Râteau .	12,369	,,	,,

TABLE OF HEIGHTS—*continued.*

Name	Height in feet	Authority	Method
PEAKS			
Crête de la Bérarde .	12,323	E. M. F.	△
La Grande Ruine . .	12,316	,,	,,
St. de Roche-Faurio .	12,192	,,	,,
Crête du Glacier Blanc .	12,008	,,	,,
Mont Bans, or Bans .	11,979	,,	,,
St. des Rouies .	11,923	,,	,,
Aiguille du Plat . .	11,818	,,	,,
Jocelme . . .	11,762	,,	,,
Pic d'Olan . . .	11,739	,,	,,
Montagne de Clotchâtel .	11,729	,,	,,
Tête de l'Étre . .	11,690	,,	,,
Rocher de l'Encula .	11,608	,,	,,
Aiguilles d'Arve :—			
South Peak .	11,529	,,	,,
North Peak .	11,513	,,	,,
Pic des Opillons .	11,505	,,	,,
Pic Bonvoisin .	11,503	,,	,,
Grandes Rousses :—			
North Peak . .	11,394	,,	,,
,, . .	11,391	W. M.	Bar.
South Peak .	11,394	E. M. F.	△
Pic North of Col du Sais	11,391	,,	,,
Tête des Fétoules . .	11,368	,,	,,
Roche de la Muzelle .	11,349	,,	,,
Crête des Bœufs Rouges .	11,332	,,	,,
Tête de Charrière .	11,293	,,	,,
Aiguille de Goléon .	11,250	,,	,,
La Grande Aiguille .	11,227	,,	,,
Cime du Vallon . .	11,214	,,	,,
Aiguille des Arias . .	11,158	,,	,,
PASSES.			
Col de la Casse Déserte .	11,516	W. M.	Bar.
Col de la Lauze . .	11,509	,,	,,
	11,204	F. F. T.	,,
Col des Ecrins .	11,017	T. G. B.	Aneroid
	10,991?	E. M. F.	△
Brèche de la Meije .	11,074	,,	,,
Col de la Tempe . .	10,889?	Berghaus	Bar.
	10,873	T. G. B.	Aneroid
Col du Glacier Blanc .	10,853	F. F. T.	Bar.
.	10,766	W. M.	,,
Col du Sélé . .	10,834	F. F. T.	B. P.
	10,794	W. M.	Bar.
Col de la Cavale .	10,174	,,	,,
	10,263?	E. M. F.	△
Col de Sais :—			
East Col . .	10,224	Forbes	Bar.
West Col . .	10,145	E. M. F.	△

TABLE OF HEIGHTS—*continued.*

Name	Height in feet	Authority	Method
PASSES			
Col du Loup	10,210?	E. M. F.	△
Col du Célar	10,092	,,	,,
Col de la Muande	10,036	,,	,,
Col de Cristillan	9,771	W. M.	Bar.
Col de Goléon	9,187	Joanne.	Estimate
Col de Maurin	8,767	W. M.	Bar.
Col des Arsines	8,262	Joanne.	Estimate
Col de Rillian	8,028	W. M.	Bar.
Col de Buffère	7,982	W. M.	Bar.
Col de l'Echauda	7,936	,,	,,
Col du Couard	7,330	,,	,,
Col des Sept Laux	7,197	,,	,,
Col du Lautaret	6,791	E. M. F.	△
Col des Echelles de Planpinet	5,876	,,	,,
Col de Venos	5,292	,,	,,

Note.—The above Tables are mainly compiled (with the kind permission of the Author) from those given by Mr. Tuckett, 'Alpine Journal,' Vol. I. No. IV.   The Col de la Pilatte has not yet been measured; it must be about 11,000 feet.

The following heights of other places mentioned in the work may be of interest; they are for the most part from 'The Alpine Guide.'

	Feet
St. Christophe . . .	4,823
La Bérarde . . .	5,702
La Grave	5,007
Monétier	4,898
Briançon	4,334
Ville de Vallouise . .	3,842
Châlets of Ailefroide . .	4,938
Cabane on Pelvoux (Soureillan) .	7,812
Guilestre	3,320
Gîte by Glacier Blanc .	8,366
Châlet of La Cochette Dessus .	6,713
Jodri	10,801

PRINTED BY SPOTTISWOODE AND CO., NEW-STREET SQUARE, LONDON